HYPNOTIC MINDS

ABDUL BASIT QAMAR

IN MEMORY OF MY BELOVED FATHER,

KHURSHID UZ ZAMAN

Contents

Preface · *i*

Acknowledgments · *iii*

Introduction

1.1 *A Journey through Time* · *2*

1.2 *The Purpose of "Hypnotic Minds"* · *9*

The Science of Hypnosis

2.1 *The Mechanism of Hypnotism* · *11*

2.2 *Theories Associated with Hypnotism* · *13*

2.3 *Brain Functioning during Hypnosis* · *40*

The Power of the Mind

3.1 *Understanding Subconscious* · *44*

3.2 *Hypnosis and the Interplay between Conscious and Subconscious Minds* · *50*

3.3 *Hypnosis in Therapy, Performance Enhancement, and Self-Improvement* · *55*

Techniques and Methods

4.1 How to Induce a Hypnotic State **61**

4.2 Different Methods of Hypnosis **69**

4.3 Importance of Language and Suggestion in Hypnosis **77**

The Benefits of Hypnosis

5.1 The Benefits of Hypnosis **85**

5.2 The Potential Downsides and Risks of Hypnosis **102**

5.3 The Use of Hypnosis in Different Industries **110**

Overcoming Fears and Skepticism

6.1 Common Misconceptions and Fears about Hypnosis **117**

6.2 The Ethical Considerations and Guidelines **124**

6.3 The Scientific Evidence Supporting the Effectiveness of Hypnosis **134**

Summary **139**

Notes **142**

Preface

As a psychologist, researcher, and author of "The Triumphant Mind - Success Rituals" and "The Journey of Self-discovery," I have spent much of my career exploring the mysteries of the human mind. In this book, "Hypnotic Minds," I have turned my attention to the fascinating world of hypnosis, which has captivated people for centuries and remains an area of ongoing exploration and controversy.

In "Hypnotic Minds," I have attempted to provide a comprehensive guide to hypnosis, drawing on my expertise as a psychologist and researcher as well as my experience working with clients. I have structured the book around six key topics, each of which explores a different aspect of hypnosis and its many applications and benefits.

I begin by introducing the reader to the basics of hypnosis, exploring its history and evolution, and explaining the various theories and models that have been developed to explain how it works. From there, I delve into the science of hypnosis, examining the latest research on brain function and consciousness, and how hypnosis can be used to influence behavior and cognition.

One of the most fascinating aspects of hypnosis is its ability to tap into the power of the mind, unlocking hidden resources and potential that might otherwise remain dormant. In this book, I explore the many techniques and methods used in hypnosis, from suggestion and visualization to regression and past life regression. I also provide detailed guidance on how to conduct hypnosis sessions, including how to set up a safe and comfortable environment, how to build rapport with clients, and how to tailor interventions to meet individual needs.

Throughout the book, I also discuss the many benefits of hypnosis, both for personal growth and healing. Whether you are looking to overcome anxiety or fear, quit smoking, lose weight, or simply unlock your full potential, hypnosis can be a powerful tool for achieving your goals. I draw on my own experiences working with clients to provide case studies and real-life examples of how hypnosis can be used to bring about lasting change.

But perhaps most importantly, I also address some of the common fears and misconceptions surrounding hypnosis and offer practical advice for anyone interested in exploring this fascinating field. I debunk myths about hypnosis being mind control or something that only works on weak-willed people. I discuss the importance of informed consent and ethical practice and how hypnosis should be used as a complementary and not a substitute for traditional medical treatments.

In writing this book, I hope to inspire readers to embrace the power of their minds, and to recognize the incredible potential that lies within them. I also aim to promote a deeper understanding of hypnosis and its many applications, helping to dispel some of the myths and misconceptions that continue to surround this fascinating field.

Whether you are a seasoned hypnotherapist, a curious skeptic, or simply someone looking to learn more about this topic, I believe you will find something of value in these pages. I invite you to join me on a journey of discovery, as we explore the mysteries of the hypnotic mind and discover the power of hypnosis to transform lives.

Acknowledgments

First and foremost, I would like to express my deepest gratitude to my friends and family for their unwavering support and encouragement throughout the writing process of this book. Their love and support have been invaluable and have made this journey possible.

I would also like to thank Mahnoor Shahid, for guiding me with her wisdom and expertise. Her motivational words and support have been instrumental in shaping the content of this book.

I would also like to thank the team at Kindle Direct Publishing (KDP), Amazon, for their hard work and dedication in bringing this book to life. Their expertise and professionalism have been essential in bringing this project to fruition.

Finally, I would like to express my appreciation to all of my readers. Your support and encouragement have been the driving force behind this book and I hope that it will be of value to you in your journey toward success.

Once again, thank you to everyone who has supported me throughout this process. I am deeply grateful for your contributions and support.

Introduction

Overview

❖ ***A Journey through Time***

- ✓ *The History of Hypnotism*
- ✓ *The Scientific Study of Hypnotism*
- ✓ *The Practice of Hypnotism*
- ✓ *Controversy and Criticism*

❖ ***The Purpose of "Hypnotic Minds"***

1.1 A Journey through Time

Hypnosis has been used for thousands of years for a variety of purposes, from inducing trance-like states for spiritual and medicinal purposes to helping individuals make positive changes in their lives. Despite its long history, hypnosis remains a fascinating and endlessly intriguing subject, with much still not understood about its mechanisms and effects. In this chapter, we will explore the history of hypnosis and its evolution from an ancient practice to modern-day science.

- ### *The History of Hypnotism*

The history of hypnotism can be divided into several phases, each characterized by a different understanding of what hypnosis is and how it works. The following is a brief overview of each of these phases:

✓ ### *The Mesmeric Era (the 1770s-1840s)*

This era is named after Franz Anton Mesmer, who is considered the father of modern hypnotism. He believed that the human body was influenced by a universal fluid that flowed through all things and that this fluid could be harnessed for therapeutic purposes. He used passes of the hand and magnets in his treatment, which he called "animal magnetism."

✓ ### *The Braidian Era (the 1840s-1890s)*

James Braid, an English surgeon, further developed the concept of hypnotism. He discovered that hypnotism could be induced through fixation of the gaze and suggestion, and he used it primarily for surgical anesthesia and the treatment of various medical conditions. He was the first person to use the term "hypnotism."

✓ *The Psychological Era (the 1890s-1920s)*

In this era, the use of hypnotism as a therapeutic tool became more widespread. Several notable psychologists and psychiatrists, including Sigmund Freud and Carl Jung, incorporated hypnotism into their practices, and it became a popular tool in the field of psychology.

✓ *The Contemporary Era (1920s-present)*

In the contemporary era, hypnotism has become a widely used tool in both psychology and alternative medicine. The exact mechanisms of hypnotism and the extent of its effectiveness are still the subjects of much debate among scientists and medical professionals, but it continues to be a popular tool in the field of psychology and alternative medicine.

The practice of hypnotism involves inducing a state of altered consciousness in the subject, known as a hypnotic trance. This state is characterized by increased suggestibility and a heightened state of suggestibility, and it can be used to help individuals access previously unconscious thoughts and feelings, modify behaviors and beliefs, and reduce anxiety Mind pain.

The exact nature of hypnotic trance and how it works is still the subject of much debate among scientists and medical professionals. Some view it as a state of heightened suggestibility and others view it as a unique state of consciousness that is separate from waking and sleeping. Regardless of its exact nature, hypnotism has been used to treat a variety of conditions, including anxiety, phobias, pain, and weight management, among others.

• *The Scientific Study of Hypnotism*

The scientific study of hypnotism, also known as hypnosis research, is a field of study that seeks to understand the nature and mechanisms of hypnotic trance and its effects on the human mind and body. This field of study encompasses a wide range of disciplines, including psychology, neuroscience, medicine, and sociology, and it has a long and complex history.

One of the earliest scientific studies of hypnotism was conducted in the late 19th century by psychologist and physician Hippolyte Bernheim. He was interested in the therapeutic potential of hypnotism and sought to understand the nature of hypnotic trance and how it worked. He conducted a series of experiments to test the effects of hypnotic suggestion on various physiological and psychological processes and found that hypnotic suggestion could alter a wide range of experiences, from perception to motor behavior.

In the early 20th century, psychologist and psychiatrist Sigmund Freud became interested in hypnotism and incorporated it into his practice. He believed that hypnotism could be used to access unconscious thoughts and feelings, and he used it to help patients with psychological problems. However, he later abandoned the use of hypnotism in favor of other techniques.

In the decades that followed, numerous studies were conducted to test the effectiveness of hypnotism for various medical and psychological conditions. Some of these studies found promising results, while others produced mixed or inconclusive results.

In recent years, advances in neuroscience have led to a greater understanding of the brain and its role in a hypnotic trance. For example, functional magnetic resonance imaging (fMRI) and other brain imaging techniques have been used to study the neural basis of hypnotic trance and the effects of hypnotic suggestion on the brain.

Despite these advances, the exact nature of hypnotic trance and how it works remains the subject of much debate among scientists and medical professionals. Some view it as a state of heightened suggestibility and others view it as a unique state of consciousness that is separate from waking and sleeping.

In general, the scientific study of hypnotism is an ongoing and evolving field of study, and there is still much that is not understood about this phenomenon. Nevertheless, it remains an important area of research, as a better understanding of hypnotism and its effects could lead to the development of new and effective treatments for a wide range of medical and psychological conditions.

- ### *The Practice of Hypnotism*

The practice of hypnotism involves inducing a state of altered consciousness in a person, known as a hypnotic trance. This state is characterized by increased suggestibility and a heightened state of suggestibility, and it can be used to help individuals access previously unconscious thoughts and feelings, modify behaviors and beliefs, and reduce anxiety and pain, among other things.

The hypnotic trance is usually induced through the use of suggestion, either verbally or non-verbally. The hypnotist may use techniques such as fixation of the gaze, progressive muscle relaxation, or guided imagery to help the subject achieve a state of trance.

Once the subject is in a hypnotic trance, the hypnotist may use suggestions to help the subject access unconscious thoughts and feelings, change behaviors and beliefs, or manage physical symptoms such as pain or anxiety. The exact nature of the suggestions used will depend on the specific goals of the hypnotist and the individual needs of the subject.

It's important to note that the hypnotic trance is not a state of unconsciousness, and the subject is not under the control of the hypnotist. Instead, the subject is in a state of heightened suggestibility, which allows the hypnotist to make suggestions that the subject is more likely to accept.

The practice of hypnotism is often used in a therapeutic setting, and hypnotists may be licensed mental health professionals, such as psychologists or psychiatrists, or they may be trained in hypnotism as complementary or alternative therapy.

There is still much debate among medical professionals about the effectiveness of hypnotism, and its use is not accepted by all medical professionals. Some view it as a valid therapeutic tool, while others view it as a form of pseudoscience.

Nevertheless, hypnotism remains a popular alternative or complementary therapy, and it continues to be used by many individuals for a wide range of purposes.

- ***Controversy and Criticism***

Hypnotism has been the subject of controversy and criticism since its inception. Some of the main criticisms and controversies surrounding hypnotism include:

✓ ***Scientific Validity***

Despite its widespread use, the scientific validity of hypnotism remains the subject of much debate. Some view it as a valid therapeutic tool, while others view it as a form of pseudoscience with little or no scientific evidence to support its efficacy.

✓ ***The Nature of the Hypnotic Trance***

There is still much debate among scientists and medical professionals about the exact nature of the hypnotic trance and how it works. Some view it as a state of heightened suggestibility, while others view it as a unique state of consciousness that is separate from waking and sleeping.

✓ ***The Power of Suggestion***

Critics of hypnotism argue that the effects of hypnotism are largely due to the power of suggestion and that the hypnotic trance itself is not a necessary component of the process.

✓ *Ethics and Exploitation*

There have been concerns raised about the ethics of hypnotism and the potential for hypnotists to exploit vulnerable individuals. For example, some have raised concerns about the use of hypnotism in stage performances or other entertainment settings, where the subject may be put in embarrassing or compromising situations.

✓ *Potential for Harm*

Some have raised concerns about the potential for hypnotism to cause harm, particularly in cases where the hypnotist is not properly trained or qualified. For example, some have argued that hypnotism could be used to induce false memories or alter a person's perception of reality in ways that could be harmful.

Despite these criticisms and controversies, hypnotism continues to be a popular and widely used therapy, and many individuals report significant benefits from its use. However, it's important to approach hypnotism with caution and to carefully consider the potential risks and benefits before undergoing treatment.

1.2   The Purpose of "Hypnotic Minds"

The purpose of "Hypnotic Minds" is to provide a comprehensive and engaging overview of hypnosis and its many applications. Through this book, you will gain a deeper understanding of what hypnosis is, its history and development, and how it is currently used in various settings, including therapy, personal development, and entertainment.

In this book, you can expect to learn about the different theories and techniques of hypnosis, including how to induce and maintain a hypnotic state, as well as how to use hypnosis for self-improvement and to achieve specific goals. The book will also explore the various ways in which hypnosis is used in therapy, including for the treatment of anxiety, depression, addiction, and pain management.

In addition, you will learn about the various controversies and criticisms surrounding hypnosis and will be provided with a balanced and evidence-based perspective on the potential benefits and risks associated with this powerful tool.

Ultimately, the goal of "Hypnotic Minds" is to provide you with a comprehensive and in-depth understanding of hypnosis and its many applications, and to empower them to use this knowledge to make positive changes in your life. Whether you are a professional practitioner, a curious reader, or simply someone looking to better understand this fascinating and endlessly intriguing subject, this book is an essential resource for you if you are interested to know about the power of hypnosis.

The Science of Hypnosis

Overview

❖ **The Mechanism of Hypnotism**

❖ **Theories Associated with Hypnotism**

- ✓ *The Social-Psychological Theory*
- ✓ *The Neuro-Physiological Theory*
- ✓ *The Cognitive Theory*
- ✓ *The Dissociation Theory*
- ✓ *The Cognitive-Behavioral Theory*
- ✓ *The Trance Theory*
- ✓ *The Repressed Memory Theory*
- ✓ *The Ideo-Dynamic Theory*
- ✓ *The Pain Control Theory*
- ✓ *The Multiple Code Theory*

❖ **Brain Functioning during Hypnosis**

- ✓ *Changes in Brain Activity*
- ✓ *Altered States of Consciousness*
- ✓ *Modulation of Pain Perception*
- ✓ *Increased Relaxation*
- ✓ *Increased Focus and Attention*

2.1 *The Mechanism of Hypnotism*

One of the key aspects of hypnosis is the concept of trance, which refers to the altered state of consciousness that occurs during hypnosis. This altered state is characterized by heightened suggestibility and increased responsiveness to suggestion and influence. There is an ongoing debate among researchers and practitioners about the nature of hypnotic trance, and how it is related to other states of consciousness such as sleep and meditation.

One theory of the hypnotic trance is that it is a state of focused attention, in which the individual can bypass their critical thinking and become more open to suggestion and influence. This theory is based on the idea that hypnosis involves a shift in attentional focus, which allows the individual to access previously unconscious thoughts, feelings, and behaviors. Some researchers have suggested that this shift in focus is related to changes in activity in specific regions of the brain, such as the anterior cingulate cortex, which is involved in attention and decision-making.

Another theory of hypnotic trance is the dissociation theory, which posits that hypnosis involves a separation between conscious and unconscious processes. According to this theory, the hypnotist can bypass the individual's critical thinking and directly access unconscious thoughts and feelings, allowing them to make changes at the unconscious level. Some researchers have suggested that this separation between conscious and unconscious processes is related to changes in activity in specific regions of the brain, such as the dorsolateral prefrontal cortex, which is involved in executive functions and decision-making.

There is also growing evidence to suggest that hypnosis involves changes in neurobiological processes, such as the release of specific neurotransmitters and hormones. For example, some studies have found that hypnosis is associated with changes in the levels of hormones such as cortisol, which is involved in stress and immune function. Other studies have found that hypnosis is associated with changes in neurotransmitters such as dopamine, which is involved in motivation and reward. These changes in neurobiological processes are thought to play a role in the mechanism of hypnosis, and to be related to the altered state of consciousness that occurs during the hypnotic trance.

It is important to note that the specific techniques used by the hypnotist can also play a role in the mechanism of hypnosis. For example, the use of suggestion, imagery, and other forms of hypnotic induction can help to focus the individual's attention and increase their suggestibility. These techniques can also help to activate specific regions of the brain, such as the anterior cingulate cortex and the dorsolateral prefrontal cortex, which are involved in attention and decision-making.

In conclusion, the exact mechanism of hypnosis is still not fully understood, and there is ongoing scientific debate about how it works. However, it is widely agreed that hypnosis involves changes in attention, suggestibility, and consciousness and that it can be used to help individuals access previously unconscious thoughts, feelings, and behaviors. Further research is needed to fully understand the underlying mechanisms of hypnosis, and to determine the best ways to use it for therapeutic and other purposes.

2.2 Theories Associated with Hypnotism

There are several different theories of hypnosis, each of which offers a unique perspective on how hypnosis works and why it is effective. Some of the most commonly discussed theories of hypnosis include:

• *The Social-Psychological Theory*

The social-psychological theory of hypnosis is one of the most widely accepted explanations for the phenomenon of hypnosis. According to this theory, hypnosis is a form of social influence that occurs between the hypnotist and the individual being hypnotized.

The social-psychological theory of hypnosis emphasizes the role of suggestion and expectations in the hypnotic experience. According to this theory, the hypnotist's suggestions and expectations, as well as the individual's expectations, play a crucial role in shaping the hypnotic experience. For example, if the hypnotist suggests that the individual will feel more relaxed during hypnosis, the individual is likely to experience a state of increased relaxation. If the individual has a positive expectation about the outcome of the hypnosis session, they are more likely to experience a positive outcome.

This theory also emphasizes the role of social cues and nonverbal communication in the hypnotic experience. For example, the hypnotist may use specific gestures, tone of voice, or eye movements to help the individual enter a hypnotic trance. These social cues can help to create a sense of rapport and trust between the hypnotist and the individual and can make it easier for the hypnotist to communicate suggestions and expectations to the individual.

The social-psychological theory of hypnosis also takes into account the individual's motivations and beliefs about hypnosis. For example, if the individual has positive expectations and beliefs about hypnosis, they are more likely to have a positive hypnotic experience. On the other hand, if the individual has negative expectations and beliefs about hypnosis, they are more likely to resist the hypnotist's suggestions and have a negative experience.

✓ *Strengths of the Social-psychological theory*

1. Explanation of the role of suggestion and expectations

The social-psychological theory of hypnosis provides a clear explanation for the role of suggestion and expectations in the hypnotic experience. This helps to understand why hypnosis can be an effective tool for change and why it is so important to tailor the hypnotic experience to the individual's specific needs, motivations, and expectations.

2. Emphasis on the importance of nonverbal communication

The social-psychological theory of hypnosis highlights the importance of nonverbal communication in the hypnotic experience. This helps to explain why the hypnotist's gestures, tone of voice, and eye movements can play a crucial role in shaping the hypnotic experience.

3. Consideration of individual differences

The social-psychological theory of hypnosis takes into account individual differences in motivations, beliefs, and expectations. This helps to explain why some individuals are more susceptible to hypnosis than others, and why some individuals have more positive hypnotic experiences than others.

✓ *Limitations of the Social-psychological theory*

1. Limited explanation of the neural mechanisms of hypnosis

While the social-psychological theory of hypnosis provides a useful framework for understanding the role of suggestion and expectations in the hypnotic experience, it does not provide a comprehensive explanation for the underlying neural mechanisms of hypnosis.

2. Emphasis on the hypnotist's role

The social-psychological theory of hypnosis places a great deal of emphasis on the role of the hypnotist in shaping the hypnotic experience. This can make it difficult to understand the individual's own internal processes and motivations that contribute to the hypnotic experience.

3. Limitations in explaining the experience of hypnotic trance

While the social-psychological theory of hypnosis provides a useful framework for understanding the role of suggestion and expectations in the hypnotic experience, it does not provide a comprehensive explanation for the subjective experience of the hypnotic trance.

In conclusion, the social-psychological theory of hypnosis provides a useful framework for understanding the role of suggestion, expectations, and social cues in the hypnotic experience. However, it is important to acknowledge its limitations and consider other theories and approaches to have a more complete understanding of hypnosis.

• *The Neuro-Physiological Theory*

The neuro-physiological theory of hypnosis is a scientific approach that seeks to understand the underlying neural mechanisms of hypnosis. This theory views hypnosis as a state of consciousness that is characterized by changes in brain activity and function.

According to the neuro-physiological theory of hypnosis, hypnosis is associated with changes in brain activity in several key regions, including the frontal cortex, the basal ganglia, and the anterior cingulate cortex. These changes in brain activity are thought to be responsible for the characteristic features of hypnosis, such as increased suggestibility and altered perception.

Research in this field has used neuroimaging techniques, such as functional magnetic resonance imaging (fMRI) and electroencephalography (EEG), to study brain activity during hypnosis. This research has found that during hypnosis, there is increased activity in certain regions of the brain, such as the frontal cortex, and decreased activity in others, such as the parietal cortex.

One of the key findings of neuro-physiological research on hypnosis is that the hypnotic state is associated with increased activity in the frontal cortex, which is involved in executive control and attention. This increased activity in the frontal cortex is thought to allow the individual to concentrate and focus more easily, and to be more receptive to suggestions from the hypnotist.

Another key finding is that hypnosis is associated with decreased activity in the parietal cortex, which is involved in processing sensory information and spatial awareness. This decrease in activity in the parietal cortex is thought to be responsible for the altered perception and experiences that occur during hypnosis, such as feelings of floating or detachment from the body.

✓ *Strengths of the Neuro-physiological theory*

1. *The scientific explanation for hypnosis*

The neuro-physiological theory of hypnosis provides a scientific explanation for the underlying mechanisms of hypnosis. This helps to increase our understanding of hypnosis and to provide a basis for further research in this field.

2. *Improved understanding of brain activity during hypnosis*

The use of neuroimaging techniques in research on hypnosis

has greatly increased our understanding of the changes in brain activity that occur during hypnosis. This has provided new insights into the nature of hypnosis and has helped to further our understanding of the brain more broadly.

3. *Improved understanding of the hypnotic state*

The neuro-physiological theory of hypnosis helps to explain the subjective experiences of hypnosis, such as increased suggestibility and altered perception. This helps to provide a more complete understanding of hypnosis and the hypnotic state.

✓ *Limitations of the Neuro-physiological theory*

1. *Limited understanding of the subjective experiences of hypnosis*

While the neuro-physiological theory of hypnosis provides a scientific explanation for the changes in brain activity that occur during hypnosis, it does not fully explain the subjective experiences of hypnosis, such as feelings of detachment or altered perception.

2. *Limited ability to explain the role of suggestion and expectations*

The neuro-physiological theory of hypnosis provides a scientific explanation for the changes in brain activity that occur during hypnosis, but it does not fully explain the role of suggestion and expectations in the hypnotic experience.

3. Limited ability to explain individual differences in susceptibility to hypnosis

While the neuro-physiological theory of hypnosis provides a scientific explanation for the changes in brain activity that occur during hypnosis, it does not fully explain why some individuals are more susceptible to hypnosis than others.

In conclusion, the neuro-physiological theory of hypnosis provides a scientific explanation for the underlying neural mechanisms of hypnosis. This theory offers important insights into the nature of hypnosis and the changes in brain activity that occur during hypnosis. However, it is important to acknowledge its limitations and consider other theories and approaches to have a more complete understanding of hypnosis.

• The Cognitive Theory

The cognitive theory of hypnosis is a psychological approach that views hypnosis as a state of heightened suggestibility and increased attentional focus. This theory proposes that hypnosis is a result of the individual's beliefs, expectations, and thoughts, rather than any physiological changes in the brain.

According to the cognitive theory of hypnosis, hypnosis is a state of consciousness that is characterized by increased attentional focus and heightened suggestibility. This increased attentional focus allows the individual to concentrate on the hypnotist's suggestions and to be more receptive to them. The heightened suggestibility allows the individual to adopt the hypnotist's suggestions as their own and to act on them.

One of the key components of the cognitive theory of hypnosis is the role of expectations and beliefs. This theory proposes that the individual's expectations and beliefs about hypnosis play a crucial role in the hypnotic experience. For example, individuals who believe that hypnosis is a powerful and effective tool are more likely to experience a strong hypnotic response than individuals who do not believe in hypnosis.

The cognitive theory of hypnosis also emphasizes the role of mental processes, such as imagination, in the hypnotic experience. This theory suggests that the individual's ability to imagine or visualize the suggestions provided by the hypnotist is an important factor in determining the success of hypnosis.

✓ ***Strengths of the Cognitive theory***

1. *Emphasis on the role of beliefs and expectations*

The cognitive theory of hypnosis emphasizes the role of beliefs and expectations in the hypnotic experience, which provides a useful framework for understanding why some individuals are more susceptible to hypnosis than others.

2. *The explanation for the role of mental processes*

The cognitive theory of hypnosis highlights the role of mental processes, such as imagination, in the hypnotic experience. This provides a useful explanation for how hypnosis can influence an individual's behavior and thoughts.

3. *Integration with other psychological theories*

The cognitive theory of hypnosis can be integrated with other psychological theories, such as cognitive-behavioral theory, which can help to provide a more comprehensive explanation for the hypnotic experience.

✓ *Limitations of the Cognitive theory*

1. *The limited explanation for physiological changes*

The cognitive theory of hypnosis focuses on the role of beliefs and expectations in the hypnotic experience but does not provide a full explanation for the physiological changes that occur during hypnosis.

2. *Limited empirical support*

While the cognitive theory of hypnosis is a well-established theoretical framework, there is limited empirical support for some of its specific claims and propositions.

3. *Lack of consensus among researchers*

There is some disagreement among researchers regarding the specific mechanisms and processes involved in hypnosis, which limits the overall strength and validity of the cognitive theory of hypnosis.

In conclusion, the cognitive theory of hypnosis provides a useful framework for understanding the role of beliefs, expectations, and mental processes in the hypnotic experience. While this theory has some limitations, it is a well-established theoretical framework that can be integrated with other psychological theories to provide a more comprehensive explanation for hypnosis.

• *The Dissociation Theory*

The dissociation theory of hypnosis is a psychological approach that views hypnosis as a state of consciousness characterized by a division or separation of various mental processes. This theory proposes that hypnosis involves a division between the individual's conscious awareness and unconscious processes, leading to a state of heightened suggestibility and altered perceptions.

According to the dissociation theory of hypnosis, hypnosis involves a division between the individual's conscious and unconscious processes, allowing the hypnotist to communicate directly with the individual's unconscious mind. This division results in a state of heightened suggestibility, in which the individual is more receptive to the hypnotist's suggestions.

One of the key components of the dissociation theory of hypnosis is the role of dissociation, which refers to the division or separation of various mental processes. This theory proposes that the individual's conscious awareness and unconscious processes are separated during hypnosis, allowing the hypnotist to communicate directly with the unconscious mind.

The dissociation theory of hypnosis also emphasizes the role of altered perceptions in the hypnotic experience. This theory suggests that hypnosis can alter an individual's perceptions and experiences, leading to changes in their thoughts, feelings, and behaviors.

✓ *Strengths of the Dissociation theory*

1. The explanation for altered perceptions

The dissociation theory of hypnosis provides a useful explanation for the altered perceptions and experiences that occur during hypnosis. This theory suggests that hypnosis involves a division between the individual's conscious and unconscious processes, leading to a state of heightened suggestibility and altered perceptions.

2. Emphasis on the role of the unconscious mind

The dissociation theory of hypnosis emphasizes the role of the unconscious mind in the hypnotic experience, which provides a useful framework for understanding why some individuals are more susceptible to hypnosis than others.

3. Integration with other psychological theories

The dissociation theory of hypnosis can be integrated with other psychological theories, such as psychodynamic theory, which can help to provide a more comprehensive explanation for the hypnotic experience.

✓ *Limitations of the Dissociation theory*

1. Limited empirical support

While the dissociation theory of hypnosis is a well-established theoretical framework, there is limited empirical support for some of its specific claims and propositions.

2.   Lack of consensus among researchers

There is some disagreement among researchers regarding the specific mechanisms and processes involved in hypnosis, which limits the overall strength and validity of the dissociation theory of hypnosis.

3.   The limited explanation for physiological changes

The dissociation theory of hypnosis focuses on the role of dissociation and altered perceptions in the hypnotic experience but does not provide a full explanation for the physiological changes that occur during hypnosis.

In conclusion, the dissociation theory of hypnosis provides a useful framework for understanding the role of the unconscious mind and altered perceptions in the hypnotic experience. While this theory has some limitations, it is a well-established theoretical framework that can be integrated with other psychological theories to provide a more comprehensive explanation for hypnosis.

• *The Cognitive-Behavioral Theory*

The cognitive-behavioral theory of hypnosis is a psychological approach that views hypnosis as a learned, voluntary behavior that is based on cognitive and behavioral processes. This theory proposes that hypnosis is a set of skills that can be learned and utilized to achieve specific goals, such as reducing anxiety, improving performance, and managing pain.

According to the cognitive-behavioral theory of hypnosis, hypnosis is a learned, voluntary behavior that involves a set of cognitive and behavioral processes, including attentional focus, suggestion, and response expectancy. The theory suggests that hypnosis works by changing the way that an individual thinks and behaves, leading to changes in their experiences and outcomes.

One of the key components of the cognitive-behavioral theory of hypnosis is the role of attentional focus, which refers to the individual's ability to direct their attention in a specific manner. This theory proposes that hypnosis works by directing the individual's attention away from their external environment and towards their internal experience, leading to changes in their thoughts, feelings, and behaviors.

The cognitive-behavioral theory of hypnosis also emphasizes the role of suggestion in the hypnotic experience. This theory suggests that the hypnotist's suggestions can influence the individual's thoughts, feelings, and behaviors, leading to changes in their experiences and outcomes.

✓ *Strengths of the Cognitive-Behavioral theory*

1. Emphasis on the role of cognition and behavior

The cognitive-behavioral theory of hypnosis emphasizes the role of cognitive and behavioral processes in the hypnotic experience, which provides a useful framework for understanding how hypnosis works.

2. Integration with other psychological theories

The cognitive-behavioral theory of hypnosis can be integrated with other psychological theories, such as social learning theory and operant conditioning, which can help to provide a more comprehensive explanation for the hypnotic experience.

3. Evidence-based approach

The cognitive-behavioral theory of hypnosis is based on empirical research, which provides a solid foundation for understanding the hypnotic experience and how it works.

4. Relevance to real-world applications

The cognitive-behavioral theory of hypnosis has practical applications in areas such as therapy, performance enhancement, and pain management, which highlights its relevance and usefulness in real-world settings.

✓ Limitations of the Cognitive-Behavioral theory

1. The limited explanation for altered perceptions

The cognitive-behavioral theory of hypnosis focuses on the role of cognition and behavior in the hypnotic experience but does not provide a full explanation for the altered perceptions that occur during hypnosis.

2. Lack of consensus among researchers

There is some disagreement among researchers regarding the

specific cognitive and behavioral processes involved in hypnosis, which limits the overall strength and validity of the cognitive-behavioral theory of hypnosis.

3. *Limited emphasis on the role of unconscious processes*

The cognitive-behavioral theory of hypnosis emphasizes the role of conscious processes, such as attentional focus and suggestion, but does not fully address the role of unconscious processes in the hypnotic experience.

In conclusion, the cognitive-behavioral theory of hypnosis provides a useful framework for understanding the role of cognition and behavior in the hypnotic experience. While this theory has some limitations, it is a well-established theoretical framework that can be integrated with other psychological theories to provide a more comprehensive explanation for hypnosis.

- ### *The Trance Theory*

The trance theory of hypnosis is a psychological approach that views hypnosis as a state of consciousness that is distinct from normal waking consciousness. According to this theory, hypnosis is a form of trance that is characterized by a set of specific physiological, psychological, and behavioral changes that are associated with alterations in awareness and attention.

The trance theory proposes that hypnosis is a state of consciousness in which the individual's attention is narrowed and focused, and their critical thinking is diminished. This state of consciousness is thought to be a result of the individual's increased suggestibility and responsiveness to the hypnotist's suggestions.

The trance theory of hypnosis also emphasizes the role of the hypnotist in inducing and maintaining the hypnotic state. The hypnotist is seen as an authority figure who provides guidance and support to the individual as they enter into and remain in the hypnotic state.

One of the key components of the trance theory of hypnosis is the concept of trance logic, which refers to the individual's acceptance of seemingly irrational or absurd suggestions during hypnosis. According to this theory, the hypnotic state allows individuals to bypass their critical thinking processes and accept suggestions that they would normally reject.

✓ *Strengths of the Trance theory*

1. Emphasis on the unique nature of the hypnotic state

The trance theory of hypnosis emphasizes the unique nature of hypnosis as a distinct state of consciousness, which provides a useful framework for understanding the hypnotic experience.

2. Explanation of altered perceptions

The trance theory of hypnosis explains the altered perceptions and experiences that occur during hypnosis, such as heightened suggestibility and responsiveness to suggestions.

3. Emphasis on the role of the hypnotist

The trance theory of hypnosis highlights the role of the

hypnotist in inducing and maintaining the hypnotic state, which provides a useful framework for understanding the therapeutic relationship between the hypnotist and the individual.

4.   Integration with other theories

The trance theory of hypnosis can be integrated with other psychological theories, such as cognitive-behavioral theory and neuro-physiological theory, to provide a more comprehensive explanation for hypnosis.

✓   Limitations of the Trance theory

1.   Limited empirical support

There is limited empirical research to support the specific physiological, psychological, and behavioral changes that are associated with the hypnotic state, which limits the overall strength of the trance theory of hypnosis.

2.   Lack of consensus among researchers

There is some disagreement among researchers regarding the specific characteristics and criteria for defining the hypnotic state, which limits the validity of the trance theory of hypnosis.

3.   The limited explanation for individual differences

The trance theory of hypnosis does not fully address the individual differences in susceptibility to hypnosis, which limits its overall usefulness as a theoretical framework.

4. *Emphasis on the hypnotist's role*

The trance theory of hypnosis emphasizes the role of the hypnotist in inducing and maintaining the hypnotic state but does not fully address the role of the individual in the hypnotic experience.

In conclusion, the trance theory of hypnosis provides a useful framework for understanding the unique nature of hypnosis as a distinct state of consciousness. While this theory has some limitations, it is a well-established theoretical framework that can be integrated with other psychological theories to provide a more comprehensive explanation for hypnosis.

- ### *The Repressed Memory Theory*

The repressed memory theory of hypnosis is the idea that traumatic experiences can be repressed from conscious memory and then retrieved during hypnosis. This theory suggests that hypnosis can be used to uncover repressed memories of traumatic events that may have been unconsciously suppressed, leading to psychological and behavioral problems.

✓ *Strengths of the Repressed Memory theory*

1. *Explanation of psychological disorders*

The repressed memory theory explains some psychological disorders, such as post-traumatic stress disorder (PTSD), by suggesting that they may result from repressed traumatic memories.

2. *Explanation of psychological disorders*

The repressed memory theory highlights the potential therapeutic benefits of hypnosis, by suggesting that it can be used to uncover and process repressed traumatic memories.

3. *Explanation of psychological disorders*

The repressed memory theory suggests that behavioral problems, such as phobias and anxiety, may result from unconsciously suppressed traumatic memories, which can be retrieved during hypnosis.

✓ *Limitations of the Repressed Memory theory*

1. *Limited empirical support*

There is limited empirical research to support the idea that traumatic memories can be repressed and then retrieved during hypnosis.

2. *Possibility of false memories*

The use of hypnosis to retrieve repressed memories is controversial, as it can also lead to the creation of false memories, which can have negative consequences for the individual.

3. Disagreement among experts

There is disagreement among experts about the validity and reliability of repressed memory theory, with some experts questioning the accuracy and authenticity of memories retrieved through hypnosis.

4. Criticism from legal perspectives

The use of hypnosis to retrieve repressed memories has been criticized from a legal perspective, as it has been used as evidence in court cases, but the reliability and accuracy of such memories are often called into question.

In conclusion, the repressed memory theory of hypnosis suggests that traumatic memories can be repressed and then retrieved during hypnosis. While this theory has some potential therapeutic benefits, it is also controversial and has been criticized for the potential to create false memories. Further empirical research is needed to determine the validity and reliability of this theory.

• The Ideo-Dynamic Theory

The Ideo-Dynamic Theory of hypnosis is a psychological theory that suggests that hypnosis works by allowing individuals to tap into their unconscious mind and access their internal motivations and desires. According to this theory, hypnosis acts as a bridge between the conscious and unconscious mind, enabling the individual to access and utilize their unconscious resources.

✓ *Strengths of the Ideo-Dynamic theory*

1. *Emphasis on the role of the unconscious mind*

The Ideo-Dynamic Theory places a strong emphasis on the role of the unconscious mind in hypnosis and suggests that it is through accessing the unconscious mind that individuals can make positive changes in their behavior and attitudes.

2. *Explanation of hypnotic suggestibility*

The Ideo-Dynamic Theory explains why some individuals are more susceptible to hypnosis than others, by suggesting that their unconscious desires and motivations are more easily accessible.

3. *Potential for personal growth*

By accessing their unconscious mind, the Ideo-Dynamic Theory suggests that individuals can uncover their unconscious motivations and desires, leading to greater self-awareness and personal growth.

✓ *Limitations of the Ideo-Dynamic theory*

1. *Lack of empirical support*

There is limited empirical research to support the Ideo-Dynamic Theory, and it is not as widely accepted as some of the other theories of hypnosis.

2. *Vagueness of the theory*

The Ideo-Dynamic Theory can be seen as vague and difficult to quantify, making it challenging to test and evaluate its validity.

3. *Potential for manipulation*

The emphasis on accessing the unconscious mind through hypnosis raises concerns about the potential for manipulation, as individuals may be induced to act in ways that are not in their best interests.

4. *Difficulty in replication*

The subjective nature of the Ideo-Dynamic Theory can make it difficult to replicate and verify its findings scientifically.

In conclusion, the Ideo-Dynamic Theory of hypnosis suggests that hypnosis allows individuals to access their unconscious mind and utilize their internal motivations and desires to make positive changes in their behavior and attitudes. While this theory has some potential benefits, it is also limited by its lack of empirical support and the potential for manipulation.

- ### *The Pain Control Theory*

The Pain Control Theory of hypnosis suggests that hypnosis can be used to control and manage physical pain. This theory suggests that hypnosis works by altering the individual's perception of pain and decreasing the amount of pain they experience.

✓ Strengths of the Pain Control theory

1. Clinical applications

The Pain Control Theory of hypnosis has practical applications in the medical field, where it can be used as a non-invasive and drug-free method for managing pain.

2. Evidence-based

There is a growing body of evidence to support the effectiveness of hypnosis in pain management, including both anecdotal reports and empirical research.

3. Potential for reducing the need for pain medications

By reducing the amount of pain experienced, the Pain Control Theory of hypnosis suggests that it could reduce the need for pain medications, which can have negative side effects and may be addictive.

✓ Limitations of the Pain Control theory

1. Limited evidence

While there is some evidence to support the effectiveness of hypnosis in pain management, the evidence is not yet conclusive and more research is needed to fully understand its mechanism of action.

2. Individual variability

The effectiveness of hypnosis in pain management may vary from person to person, depending on factors such as the individual's level of hypnotizability and the nature of the pain being experienced.

3. Lack of standardization

There is currently a lack of standardization in the use of hypnosis for pain management, making it difficult to compare results between studies and ensure consistent outcomes.

4. Controversy

The use of hypnosis for pain management remains a controversial issue, with some skeptics challenging its effectiveness and the mechanisms by which it is thought to work.

In conclusion, the Pain Control Theory of hypnosis suggests that hypnosis can be used as an effective method for controlling and managing physical pain. While this theory has some potential benefits, it is also limited by the lack of conclusive evidence and the individual variability in its effectiveness. Nevertheless, the use of hypnosis for pain management remains an area of interest and active research, and its potential as a non-invasive and drug-free method for pain management is worth exploring further.

- ### The Multiple Code Theory

The Multiple Code Theory of hypnosis is a theory that suggests that hypnosis is not a single, unitary phenomenon, but rather a complex and multi-faceted process that involves multiple cognitive, affective, and physiological systems. According to this theory, hypnosis is a result of the interplay between these multiple systems, which work together to produce the trance-like state associated with hypnosis.

✓ *Strengths of the Multiple Code theory*

1. *Explanation of the complexity of hypnosis*

The Multiple Code Theory offers a comprehensive explanation of the complex and multi-faceted nature of hypnosis and the role of multiple systems in the process of hypnosis.

2. *Recognition of the diversity of hypnosis*

This theory acknowledges that hypnosis can manifest in a variety of forms and that the nature of hypnosis can vary depending on the individual and the context in which it is performed.

3. *Explanation of the variability of hypnotic phenomena*

The Multiple Code Theory provides a framework for understanding why different individuals may respond differently to hypnosis and why the effects of hypnosis can be variable.

4. *Empirical support*

There is some empirical evidence to support the Multiple

Code Theory, including studies that have investigated the cognitive, affective, and physiological processes involved in hypnosis.

✓ *Limitations of the Multiple Code theory*

1. Limited empirical support

While there is some evidence to support the Multiple Code Theory, the evidence is not yet conclusive, and more research is needed to fully understand the complex processes involved in hypnosis.

2. Theoretical complexity

The Multiple Code Theory is a complex theory that can be difficult to understand, even for those with a background in psychology or neuroscience.

3. Lack of standardization

There is a lack of standardization in the measurement and definition of the different processes involved in hypnosis, which can make it difficult to compare results between studies and establish consistent outcomes.

4. Controversy

The Multiple Code Theory is controversial, and there is an ongoing debate among researchers and practitioners about its validity and its ability to fully explain the nature of hypnosis.

In conclusion, the Multiple Code Theory is a comprehensive explanation of the complex and multi-faceted nature of hypnosis, which recognizes the role of multiple systems in the process of hypnosis. While this theory has some potential strengths, it is limited by the limited empirical support and the theoretical complexity of the model. Nevertheless, it is an important area of investigation, and its potential to deepen our understanding of the nature of hypnosis and its effects is worth exploring further.

2.3 Brain Functioning during Hypnosis

The brain functioning during hypnosis is an area of active research and there is still much that is not known about the specific neural mechanisms involved. However, several theories and studies suggest changes in brain activity occur during hypnosis.

• *Changes in Brain Activity*

Neuroimaging studies have used techniques such as functional magnetic resonance imaging (fMRI) and positron emission tomography (PET) to examine changes in brain activity during hypnosis. These studies have found that certain regions of the brain, such as the frontal and temporal lobes, show changes in activity during hypnosis. Additionally, changes in activity have been observed in regions associated with attention, perception, and memory, such as the anterior cingulate cortex, the insula, the dorsolateral prefrontal cortex, and the hippocampus.

• *Altered States of Consciousness*

Some researchers have suggested that hypnosis may alter the state of consciousness, leading to changes in brain activity and altered perception, attention, and memory. This theory is based on the idea that hypnosis induces an altered state of consciousness in which the individual is highly focused and open to suggestions. This altered state of consciousness is thought to be related to changes in activity in regions of the brain associated with self-awareness and attention, such as the anterior cingulate cortex and the medial prefrontal cortex.

• *Modulation of Pain Perception*

Some studies have suggested that hypnosis can modulate pain perception by altering activity in brain regions associated with pain processing, such as the anterior cingulate cortex and the insula. This theory is based on the idea that hypnosis can affect pain perception by altering the way that pain is perceived, encoded, and processed in the brain.

• *Increased Relaxation*

During hypnosis, individuals often experience deep relaxation, which has been associated with changes in brain activity in regions associated with stress and arousal, such as the amygdala and the hypothalamus. Relaxation during hypnosis is thought to be related to changes in activity in these regions, which may reduce stress and anxiety and improve overall well-being.

• *Increased Focus and Attention*

Hypnosis has been associated with increased focus and attention, which is thought to be related to changes in activity in brain regions associated with attention and executive function, such as the dorsolateral prefrontal cortex and the parietal lobe. This increased focus and attention may help individuals to better attend to suggestions and become more receptive to therapeutic interventions.

It is important to note that these findings are still preliminary and that more research is needed to fully understand the brain mechanisms involved in hypnosis. Additionally, different studies may find different results, as the precise nature of the changes in brain activity during hypnosis may vary depending on the individual and the context in which hypnosis is performed.

In conclusion, the study of brain functioning during hypnosis is a complex and ongoing area of research, but current evidence suggests that hypnosis may involve changes in brain activity and altered states of consciousness, which may contribute to its effects on perception, attention, memory, and pain.

The Power of the Mind

Overview

❖ **Understanding Subconscious**

    ✓ *Behaviors and Hypnosis*
    ✓ *Decision-making and Hypnosis*

❖ **Hypnosis and the Interplay between Conscious and Subconscious Minds**

    ✓ *The Conscious and Subconscious Mind*
    ✓ *Accessing the Subconscious through Hypnosis*
    ✓ *Maximizing the Potential of Hypnosis*

❖ **Hypnosis in Therapy, Performance Enhancement, and Self-Improvement**

    ✓ *Hypnosis in Therapy*
    ✓ *Hypnosis in Performance Enhancement*
    ✓ *Hypnosis in Self-Improvement*

3.1 Understanding Subconscious

The concept of the subconscious mind has been a topic of fascination for centuries, with many theories and perspectives on what it is and how it functions. One common definition of the subconscious is that it is a part of the mind that operates outside of conscious awareness, but influences thoughts, emotions, and behaviors.

During hypnosis, the hypnotist's suggestions are thought to target this unconscious mind, bypassing the critical thinking of the conscious mind. To achieve this, the hypnotist often induces a state of heightened suggestibility in the individual, in which they are more open to accepting and acting on the hypnotist's suggestions.

Recent advances in neuroscience have shed light on the brain mechanisms involved in hypnosis and communication with the subconscious mind. Brain imaging studies have shown that hypnosis is associated with changes in the activity of brain regions that play a role in self-referential processing, attention and executive control, pain regulation, emotions, and memory.

For example, studies using functional magnetic resonance imaging (fMRI) have shown that hypnosis is associated with increased activity in the medial prefrontal cortex, which is involved in self-referential processing, and the anterior cingulate cortex, which plays a role in attention and executive control. Additionally, hypnosis has been shown to impact the activity of brain regions involved in the regulation of pain perception, such as the anterior insula and the rostral anterior cingulate cortex, suggesting that hypnosis may be used as a tool for pain management.

The Limbic system, which includes the amygdala and the hippocampus, is also thought to play a role in the process of hypnosis. The Limbic system is involved in the regulation of emotions, motivation, and the formation of memories, and brain imaging studies have shown that hypnosis is associated with changes in the activity of these regions.

In conclusion, the field of hypnosis is still uncovering the mysteries of the subconscious mind and how it can be influenced. However, the available evidence suggests that hypnosis is a powerful tool that can be used to target the unconscious mind and effect changes in thoughts, emotions, and behaviors. Brain imaging studies have shed light on the specific brain regions involved in this process, and future research will likely continue to shed light on the complex interplay between the conscious and unconscious mind during hypnosis.

- ### *Behaviors and Hypnosis*

The connection between behaviors and hypnosis is a complex and multifaceted one, rooted in our understanding of the role that the subconscious mind plays in shaping our daily lives. To better understand this connection, it is important to first explore the concept of the subconscious mind and how it influences our behavior.

The subconscious mind is a vast and complex network of beliefs, thoughts, emotions, and behaviors that exist below the level of conscious awareness. It is responsible for driving much of our daily behavior and habits and is often the source of negative patterns that we struggle to change. Because the subconscious mind operates outside of our conscious awareness, it can be difficult to directly access and modify its thought patterns and behaviors.

Hypnosis is a state of altered consciousness in which the mind is more suggestible to suggestions and ideas. In this state, individuals are more open to accepting and integrating new beliefs and behaviors into their subconscious minds. By accessing the subconscious mind through hypnosis, individuals can directly target and change negative thought patterns and behaviors, as well as reinforce positive habits and behaviors.

One of the key benefits of using hypnosis as a tool for behavior modification is that it allows individuals to bypass the conscious mind and directly address the root cause of negative patterns of thought and behavior. This is particularly important for individuals who have tried other methods of behavior modification without success, as it allows them to access and modify the underlying negative beliefs and habits that are holding them back.

In addition to changing negative patterns of behavior, hypnosis can also be used to reinforce positive habits and behaviors. For example, individuals may use hypnosis to help them develop a stronger sense of self-confidence, overcome performance anxiety, or to cultivate healthier habits such as exercise or a balanced diet.

It is important to note that the effectiveness of hypnosis as a tool for behavior modification can vary greatly depending on the individual and their specific needs and goals. Additionally, the quality and experience of the hypnotist can also play a significant role in the success of hypnosis as a tool for behavior modification.

Despite these factors, many individuals and therapists have found hypnosis to be a highly effective tool for behavior modification and personal transformation. Whether you are looking to overcome negative patterns of thought and behavior, or to cultivate positive habits and behaviors, hypnosis can be an effective tool for personal growth and change.

In conclusion, the connection between behaviors and hypnosis is a complex and multifaceted one, rooted in our understanding of the role that the subconscious mind plays in shaping our daily lives. By accessing the subconscious mind through hypnosis, individuals can directly target and change negative thought patterns and behaviors, as well as reinforce positive habits and behaviors. Whether you are seeking to overcome a negative pattern of behavior or to cultivate positive habits and behaviors, hypnosis can be a valuable tool for personal growth and transformation.

- ### *Decision-making and Hypnosis*

The connection between decision-making and hypnosis is complex and multi-faceted, as it involves the interplay between the conscious and subconscious mind, as well as the influence of emotions, beliefs, and past experiences on our thoughts and behaviors.

The subconscious mind is a powerful force that drives much of our daily experiences, including our decision-making processes. It is responsible for shaping our habits, attitudes, and behaviors, and it can hold onto limiting beliefs and negative thought patterns that can prevent us from making effective decisions. For example, an individual may have a the belief that they are not capable of making good decisions or that they are not deserving of success, which can result in indecision, procrastination, or self-sabotage.

Hypnosis provides a powerful tool for accessing the subconscious mind and addressing these limiting beliefs and negative patterns of behavior. During hypnosis, an individual enters into a state of altered consciousness in which they are more suggestible to suggestions and ideas. In this state, individuals can gain deeper insight into their motivations, values, and desires, and they can directly target and replace limiting beliefs with positive, empowering thoughts and behaviors.

For example, an individual may use hypnosis to gain clarity on their goals and priorities and to develop a clearer sense of direction and purpose. This can help them to make more informed and effective decisions, as they are better able to align their actions with their values and aspirations.

In addition, hypnosis can also help individuals to overcome indecision and procrastination, and to develop habits of making effective and well-considered decisions. For instance, an individual may use hypnosis to address negative patterns of behavior, such as impulsiveness or self-sabotage, and to replace these patterns with positive, empowering habits of decision-making.

It is important to note that the effectiveness of hypnosis as a tool for decision-making varies greatly depending on the individual and their specific needs and goals. Additionally, the quality and experience of the hypnotist can also play a significant role in the success of hypnosis as a tool for decision-making.

In conclusion, the relationship between decision-making and hypnosis is complex and multi-layered, involving the interplay between the conscious and subconscious mind, as well as the influence of emotions, beliefs, and past experiences on our thoughts and behaviors. Through hypnosis, individuals can gain deeper insight into their motivations, values, and desires, and they can overcome limiting beliefs and negative patterns of behavior that may be preventing them from making effective decisions. Whether you are seeking to clarify your goals, address negative patterns of behavior, or make better decisions, hypnosis can be a valuable tool for personal growth and transformation.

3.2 Hypnosis and the Interplay between Conscious and Subconscious Minds

Hypnosis is a state of altered consciousness that allows individuals to tap into their subconscious mind and make lasting changes to their thoughts, behaviors, and experiences. This unique state of mind can be induced through guided meditation or suggestion, and it is believed to be a powerful tool for personal growth and transformation. To fully understand the potential of hypnosis, it is essential to understand the relationship between the conscious and subconscious mind and how hypnosis can be used to access the deeper workings of the mind.

- ### *The Conscious and Subconscious Mind*

The conscious and subconscious mind are two distinct aspects of our mental landscape that work together to shape our thoughts, behaviors, and experiences.

4. The Conscious Mind

The conscious mind is a critical part of our mental functioning and is responsible for many important cognitive processes. When we are awake and aware, the conscious mind is active, allowing us to reflect on our thoughts, emotions, and behaviors, as well as make decisions and engage in critical thinking. This part of our mind is essential for our self-awareness and is closely tied to our sense of self.

However, despite its importance, the conscious mind is limited in its processing abilities. At any given time, it can only process a small amount of information, making it difficult to access the deeper workings of the subconscious mind. The subconscious mind, on the other hand, is responsible for the vast majority of our thoughts, emotions, and behaviors. It operates on autopilot and is responsible for our instincts, habits, and deeply ingrained patterns of thinking and behavior.

This difference in processing ability between the conscious and subconscious mind is what makes lasting change so challenging. To make significant changes to our thoughts, emotions, and behaviors, we need to be able to access and modify the underlying patterns and beliefs stored in the subconscious mind. This is where hypnosis can be especially helpful, as it provides a way to bypass the limitations of the conscious mind and directly access the subconscious mind to make lasting changes.

5. *The Subconscious Mind*

The subconscious mind is a crucial aspect of our mental landscape that shapes a large portion of our experiences, thoughts, emotions, and behaviors. Unlike the conscious mind, which is actively engaged when we are awake and aware, the subconscious mind operates on a deeper, more instinctual level and is primarily driven by memories and experiences from our past. This means that the subconscious mind has a powerful influence over our thoughts, emotions, and behaviors, and is responsible for many of the habits that we develop over time.

The subconscious mind can be thought of as a repository of information that we have accumulated throughout our lives, including memories, beliefs, experiences, and habits.

This information shapes our perceptions and experiences of the world and is responsible for many of our unconscious thoughts and behaviors. For example, if someone has a negative experience with a particular type of food, they may develop an aversion to it, even if they are not consciously aware of the reason. Similarly, if someone has a positive experience with exercise, they may develop a habit of engaging in physical activity regularly.

Accessing and influencing the subconscious mind can be challenging because it operates on a level that is beyond our conscious awareness. This means that it can be difficult to change our habits, thoughts, and behaviors through conscious means, as our conscious mind is limited in its ability to process information. However, hypnosis provides a unique pathway to the subconscious mind, allowing individuals to access and influence this deep-seated part of the mind in a safe and supportive environment. Through hypnosis, individuals can make lasting changes to their thoughts, emotions, and behaviors, promoting personal growth and transformation.

• *Accessing the Subconscious through Hypnosis*

The conscious mind is responsible for critical thinking and decision-making, but it is limited by its ability to only process a small amount of information at any given time. As a result, accessing and influencing the deeper workings of the subconscious mind, which drives much of our habits, behaviors, and experiences, can be challenging. This is where hypnosis comes in as a tool to access the subconscious mind and make changes to thoughts, emotions, and behaviors.

In hypnosis, the mind becomes more suggestible, making it

easier to target limiting beliefs, negative thought patterns, and behaviors. This increased suggestibility is the key to accessing the subconscious mind and making direct changes to it. For example, if someone has a phobia of spiders, they can use hypnosis to overcome their fear by directly accessing their subconscious mind and planting new, positive associations with spiders. Similarly, someone who wants to quit smoking can use hypnosis to change their subconscious associations with smoking and reinforce new, healthier habits.

It's important to note that the effectiveness of hypnosis in accessing the subconscious mind can vary from person to person and depends on several factors. Some individuals may see rapid and profound changes through hypnosis, while others may need multiple sessions to see results. The quality and experience of the hypnotist can also play a significant role in the success of hypnosis as a tool for personal growth and transformation.

To summarize, hypnosis is a tool that offers a unique pathway to the subconscious mind, allowing individuals to bypass the limitations of the conscious mind and make direct changes to their thoughts, emotions, and behaviors. While the effectiveness of hypnosis can vary, it can be a powerful tool for personal growth and transformation when used under the guidance of a qualified hypnotist.

- ***Maximizing the Potential of Hypnosis***

To maximize the potential of hypnosis as a tool for accessing the subconscious mind, it is essential to work with a trained and experienced hypnotist who can guide you through the process and support your goals. A good hypnotist will take the time to understand your specific needs and tailor their approach accordingly. They will also provide you with the tools and support you need to achieve your desired outcomes and sustain your changes over the long term.

In conclusion, the relationship between hypnosis and the conscious and subconscious mind highlights the complex interplay between our thoughts, behaviors, and experiences. By accessing the subconscious mind through hypnosis, individuals can directly target and change limiting beliefs, negative thought patterns, and behaviors and tap into the full potential of their minds. Whether you are looking to overcome fears and phobias, quit smoking, or simply become a more confident and self-assured person, hypnosis can be a valuable tool for personal growth and transformation.

3.3 *Hypnosis in Therapy, Performance Enhancement, and Self-Improvement*

Hypnosis is a state of altered consciousness that is characterized by increased suggestibility and focused attention. It has been used for centuries as a tool for therapy, performance enhancement, and self-improvement. Hypnosis works by bypassing the limitations of the conscious mind and accessing the subconscious mind, where many of our beliefs, thoughts, and behaviors are formed and stored. In this state of heightened suggestibility, the hypnotist can offer suggestions and ideas that can help individuals make direct changes to their thoughts, emotions, and behaviors.

• *Hypnosis in Therapy*

Hypnosis is a technique that has been used for therapeutic purposes for many years and is effective in treating a wide range of mental health conditions. Some of the conditions that can be treated with hypnosis include anxiety, depression, phobias, and other forms of emotional distress. The goal of hypnosis in therapy is to help individuals access their subconscious mind and make positive changes to the thoughts, emotions, and behaviors that are contributing to their mental health issues.

In a therapeutic setting, hypnosis is typically performed by a licensed mental health professional who is trained in the use of hypnotic techniques. The hypnotist serves as a guide, helping the individual to enter a state of deep relaxation and focus to access their subconscious mind. Once the individual is in this state, the hypnotist can use suggestion and visualization techniques to help the individual make changes to their thought patterns, beliefs, and behaviors.

One of the benefits of hypnosis is that it allows individuals to make changes in a safe and supportive environment. This is because the hypnotic state is a natural state of mind that can be induced through relaxation and suggestion. The hypnotic state can also help individuals to bypass their conscious mind, which is often the source of negative thought patterns and limiting beliefs. By accessing the subconscious mind, individuals can make lasting changes to their thoughts, emotions, and behaviors that can have a positive impact on their mental health.

In many cases, hypnosis can be used in conjunction with other therapeutic interventions, such as talk therapy or medication, to achieve optimal results. For example, a person who is struggling with anxiety and depression may receive talk therapy to help them process their feelings and experiences, while also receiving hypnosis to help them change negative thought patterns and manage their physical symptoms.

Finally, hypnosis can also be used as a tool for promoting self-awareness and personal growth. By accessing the subconscious mind, individuals can gain insight into their thoughts, emotions, and behaviors, and can work to make positive changes in these areas. This can lead to improved mental and emotional well-being, greater self-awareness, and an overall sense of personal growth and fulfillment.

In conclusion, hypnosis is a powerful and effective tool for treating mental health conditions and promoting personal growth. By accessing the subconscious mind and making positive changes to thought patterns, beliefs, and behaviors, individuals can experience significant improvements in their mental and emotional well-being. If you are interested in exploring hypnosis as a therapeutic option, it is important to work with a licensed mental health professional who is trained in the use of hypnotic techniques.

• *Hypnosis in Performance Enhancement*

Hypnosis is not just limited to its therapeutic applications, it can also be used as a tool for performance enhancement. This includes improving athletic performance, public speaking, and enhancing creativity. By accessing the subconscious mind, hypnosis can help individuals overcome performance anxiety and boost their confidence and self-esteem, which can lead to improved performance in various areas of life.

For athletes, hypnosis can be used to improve focus, motivation, and overall performance. By addressing any negative thought patterns or beliefs that may be affecting their performance, individuals can gain greater confidence and self-assurance, which can help them to perform at their best during competitions. Additionally, hypnosis can also be used to help athletes overcome specific performance-related fears, such as stage fright or performance anxiety. This can help them to remain calm and focused, even when performing under pressure.

For public speakers and performers, hypnosis can also be a valuable tool for overcoming performance anxiety. The subconscious mind plays a significant role in shaping an individual's beliefs and thought patterns, including those related to public speaking or performance. By addressing these beliefs and thoughts through hypnosis, individuals can become more confident and self-assured, allowing them to perform at their best in front of large audiences.

Furthermore, hypnosis can also be used to enhance creativity. By accessing the subconscious mind, individuals can tap into their inner imagination and creativity, which can help them to think more freely and creatively. This can be particularly helpful for individuals in creative fields, such as writers, artists, and musicians, who may need to overcome creative blocks or enhance their creative abilities.

In conclusion, hypnosis is a versatile tool that can be used for a variety of purposes, including performance enhancement. By accessing the subconscious mind, individuals can overcome performance anxiety, increase focus and motivation, and boost confidence and self-esteem, which can lead to improved performance in athletic, public speaking, and creative endeavors. If you are interested in using hypnosis for performance enhancement, it is important to work with a licensed mental health professional who is trained in the use of hypnotic techniques.

- ### *Hypnosis in Self-Improvement*

Hypnosis is a valuable tool for self-improvement and personal growth, allowing individuals to make meaningful changes to their thoughts, emotions, and behaviors in a safe and supportive environment. In a self-improvement setting, hypnosis can be used for a variety of purposes, including overcoming limiting beliefs and negative thought patterns, developing positive habits, and increasing self-awareness. Additionally, hypnosis can be used to support individuals in achieving specific goals, such as weight loss, quitting smoking, or reducing stress.

One of the key benefits of hypnosis in a self-improvement setting is its ability to target the root causes of negative behaviors and thought patterns. For example, if an individual is struggling with a negative thought pattern, such as low self-esteem, hypnosis can be used to access the subconscious mind and change this limiting belief. By doing so, the individual can develop a more positive self-image, leading to increased confidence and self-esteem.

Similarly, hypnosis can also be used to develop positive habits, such as improved sleep patterns, healthier eating habits, and increased exercise. By accessing the subconscious mind, individuals can overcome negative thought patterns and behaviors that are preventing them from achieving their goals and replace them with more positive habits.

Additionally, hypnosis can also be used for self-awareness and personal growth. By accessing the subconscious mind, individuals can gain a deeper understanding of their thoughts, emotions, and behaviors, which can lead to increased self-awareness and personal growth.

In conclusion, hypnosis is a powerful tool for self-improvement and personal growth. By accessing the subconscious mind, individuals can overcome limiting beliefs and negative thought patterns, develop positive habits, and increase self-awareness. Additionally, hypnosis can be used to support individuals in achieving specific goals, such as weight loss, quitting smoking, or reducing stress. If you are interested in using hypnosis for self-improvement, it is important to work with a licensed mental health professional who is trained in the use of hypnotic techniques.

Techniques and Methods

Overview

❖ **How to Induce a Hypnotic State**

- ✓ *Choose a Comfortable Environment*
- ✓ *Relaxation*
- ✓ *Focus*
- ✓ *Suggestion*
- ✓ *Emerging from the Hypnotic State*

❖ **Different Methods of Hypnosis**

- ✓ *Traditional Hypnosis*
- ✓ *Ericksonian Hypnosis*
- ✓ *Neuro-Linguistic Programming (NLP)*
- ✓ *Self-hypnosis*
- ✓ *Hypnotherapy*

❖ **Importance of Language and Suggestion in Hypnosis**

- ✓ *Embedded Commands*
- ✓ *Metaphors and Stories*
- ✓ *Positive Affirmations*
- ✓ *Future Pacing*

4.1 How to Induce a Hypnotic State

Hypnosis is a state of consciousness in which a person becomes highly suggestible and receptive to verbal or visual cues. While there are varying degrees of hypnotic states, from light to deep, inducing a hypnotic state typically involves relaxation, focus, and suggestion. If you are interested in exploring hypnosis and inducing a hypnotic state, here are some steps that may help you:

- ### Choose a Comfortable Environment

Choosing a comfortable environment is an important first step to successfully inducing a hypnotic state. The environment plays a significant role in creating a relaxed and focused mindset, which is essential for the success of the hypnosis session.

The first consideration when choosing a comfortable environment for hypnosis is to select a place that is quiet and free of distractions. This can be a challenge, particularly in a busy household or a noisy environment. It is important to identify a space that is as free of distractions as possible, and that is free from interruptions.

Electronic devices, in particular, can be a significant source of distraction, and it is important to turn off or silence all devices, including cell phones, televisions, and computers. Other people in the vicinity should be made aware that the individual is undergoing hypnosis and should be asked to respect their privacy and not disturb them.

Once a suitable space has been identified, the next step is to create an atmosphere that is peaceful and conducive to relaxation. A calm, tranquil environment can help the person to relax and focus on the hypnosis experience. The environment can be enhanced by using low-level lighting or candlelight, calming music, and soft furnishings.

The temperature of the environment should also be considered, and it is important to ensure that the space is at a comfortable temperature. The ideal temperature for hypnosis is between 68 and 72 degrees Fahrenheit. The individual should feel neither too hot nor too cold and should be dressed in comfortable clothing.

The seating or lying down arrangement is also important in creating a comfortable environment for hypnosis. The individual should be seated or lying down in a position that is comfortable and conducive to relaxation. A comfortable chair or couch that allows the person to recline slightly can be ideal for hypnosis. It is important to ensure that the seating or lying down arrangement is ergonomically sound and does not cause discomfort or distraction.

Overall, choosing a comfortable environment for hypnosis is a critical step in inducing a hypnotic state. The environment should be quiet, free of distractions, peaceful, and comfortable. Paying attention to the environment and creating a space that is conducive to relaxation can help to ensure that the individual can enter a state of deep relaxation, which is a necessary precursor to inducing a hypnotic state.

- ### *Relaxation*

Relaxation is a crucial element of hypnosis. To enter a hypnotic state, an individual must first achieve a deep state of relaxation. This is because hypnosis involves accessing the subconscious mind, and relaxation allows the individual to bypass the critical conscious mind and access the subconscious more easily.

Deep breathing is an effective technique for relaxation that can be used before and during hypnosis. The process involves inhaling slowly through the nose, filling the lungs with air, holding the breath for a few seconds, and then exhaling slowly through the mouth. Deep breathing can slow the heart rate, reduce stress and tension in the body, and promote a sense of calmness and relaxation.

Progressive muscle relaxation is another technique that can be used to achieve a state of deep relaxation. This technique involves tensing and then relaxing different muscle groups throughout the body, starting at the toes and working up to the head. By tensing and then releasing each muscle group, the body becomes more relaxed, and the individual can achieve a deep state of relaxation. This technique can help to release physical tension and create a sense of calmness in the body.

Visualization is also an effective technique for relaxation. It involves picturing a peaceful scene or image in the mind, such as a beach or mountain range, and focusing on the details of the scene. Visualization can help to calm the mind, reduce stress and anxiety, and create a sense of peace and tranquility.

Guided imagery is a technique that can be used during hypnosis to promote relaxation. It involves listening to a recording or the hypnotist's voice, which guides the individual through a series of mental images and sensations designed to promote relaxation. Guided imagery can help to reduce stress and anxiety, promote feelings of calmness and relaxation, and create a sense of well-being.

In addition to these techniques, it is also important to select a comfortable environment for hypnosis. A quiet, peaceful environment free from distractions such as electronic devices and other people can help to promote relaxation and focus. The temperature should be comfortable, and the seating or lying down arrangement should be conducive to relaxation.

Overall, relaxation is an essential component of hypnosis. By using a variety of relaxation techniques and selecting a comfortable environment for hypnosis, individuals can increase their chances of successfully entering a hypnotic state and achieving their desired goals.

- *Focus*

Focus is a key component of hypnosis that is essential to induce a hypnotic state. When an individual is focused, they can direct their attention to the hypnotist's voice or other cues, allowing them to become more receptive to hypnotic suggestions.

Various techniques can be used to improve focus during hypnosis. Visualization is one such technique. This involves creating mental images in the mind and focusing on them to induce a relaxed and focused state. By concentrating on a peaceful scene, the mind becomes more focused, and the individual can more easily enter a hypnotic state.

Another technique to improve focus during hypnosis is through the use of affirmations. Affirmations are positive statements that are repeated to oneself, such as "I am relaxed and focused" or "I am open to the power of suggestion." By repeating affirmations, the mind becomes more focused and receptive to the hypnotist's suggestions, making it easier to enter a hypnotic state.

Breathing techniques are another way to improve focus during hypnosis. Deep breathing, for instance, can help to calm the mind and slow down the heart rate, allowing the individual to become more relaxed and focused on the hypnotist's voice.

Selecting a comfortable environment for hypnosis is also important to improve focus. The environment should be quiet, peaceful, and free of distractions such as electronic devices or other people. Ideally, the environment should be conducive to relaxation and focus, allowing the individual to concentrate on the hypnotist's voice and enter a state of hypnosis more easily.

Overall, focus is a crucial element of hypnosis and using visualization, affirmations, breathing techniques, and other methods can help to improve focus during the hypnosis process. By creating a comfortable environment for hypnosis, individuals can increase their chances of successfully entering a hypnotic state and achieving their desired goals.

- ***Suggestion***

The suggestion is a fundamental principle of hypnosis that involves influencing the thoughts, feelings, and behaviors of an individual through verbal or nonverbal communication. The primary goal of suggestion is to help individuals overcome negative behaviors, thoughts, or habits, and to facilitate positive changes in their lives.

There are two main types of suggestions used in hypnosis: direct and indirect suggestions. Direct suggestions are straightforward and explicit and often involve specific commands or requests. For example, a direct suggestion for smoking cessation might be "You will no longer have any desire to smoke," or "You will feel a strong sense of confidence in your ability to quit smoking." Direct suggestions can be highly effective, especially when the individual is highly suggestible or motivated to change.

Indirect suggestions, on the other hand, are more subtle and creative, and often involve storytelling, metaphors, or other forms of indirect language. Indirect suggestions work by bypassing the conscious mind and accessing the subconscious, where they can influence behavior and thinking patterns. For example, an indirect suggestion for smoking cessation might be a story about a bird that learns to fly after overcoming obstacles and challenges, with the underlying message that the individual can overcome their addiction by persevering and taking action.

For suggestions to be effective, they must be tailored to the individual's specific needs, beliefs, and motivations. The hypnotist must take the time to understand the individual's goals and values and create suggestions that are likely to be accepted and acted upon. The hypnotist must also deliver suggestions with confidence, authority, and conviction, as this can enhance their effectiveness.

The hypnotist needs to avoid making suggestions that go against the individual's values, beliefs, or ethics. Suggesting something that is not in alignment with the individual's core values can cause them to reject the suggestion or even break the hypnotic state, rendering the hypnosis ineffective.

In summary, the suggestion is a critical component of

hypnosis and it can be used to help individuals overcome negative patterns of behavior, thoughts, or habits and facilitate positive change. The success of suggestions depends on the individual's suggestibility, the hypnotist's ability to tailor suggestions to the individual, and the delivery of suggestions with confidence and authority.

• *Emerging from the Hypnotic State*

Emerging from the hypnotic state is a crucial component of the hypnosis process as it involves bringing the individual back to their normal waking state. It is important to note that hypnosis is a trance state that the individual enters with the guidance of the hypnotist. During hypnosis, the individual is in a state of deep relaxation and heightened suggestibility. They can focus on the hypnotist's suggestions and may experience a range of physical and mental sensations.

When it is time to emerge from the hypnotic state, the hypnotist must take care to ensure that the individual makes a smooth and comfortable transition. Abruptly ending the session or bringing the individual out of hypnosis too quickly can be disorienting and may cause feelings of confusion or anxiety.

One common technique that hypnotists use to help individuals emerge from hypnosis is to count the individual out of the trance state. This involves counting from one to five or a higher number, with each number representing an increased level of alertness and energy. As the hypnotist counts, they may give suggestions to the individual to help them feel more alert and energized.

Another technique that can be used to help individuals emerge from hypnosis is to gradually introduce external stimuli, such as light or sound. This can help the individual slowly transition back to their normal waking state. For example, the hypnotist may gradually increase the volume of the music playing in the background or turn on a light in the room.

Hypnotists need to take the time to debrief with the individual after the hypnosis session. During this time, the hypnotist may discuss any experiences or insights that the individual had during the session and answer any questions they may have. This can help the individual to better understand the hypnosis process and the changes that may have occurred as a result of the session.

In conclusion, emerging from the hypnotic state is an essential part of the hypnosis process, and it requires the careful attention of the hypnotist to ensure that the individual makes a smooth and comfortable transition back to their normal waking state. With proper technique and guidance, individuals can achieve their desired goals and experience positive changes in their lives through the power of hypnosis.

4.2 Different Methods of Hypnosis

There are several different methods of hypnosis, and their effectiveness can vary depending on the individual and the goals of the hypnosis session. Here are some of the most common methods:

- ### *Traditional Hypnosis*

Traditional hypnosis is a method of hypnosis that has been in use for many years and is also known as "authoritarian" or "direct" hypnosis. In traditional hypnosis, the hypnotist uses a commanding, authoritative tone of voice and gives direct suggestions to the individual to induce a hypnotic state. The goal is to help the individual to become more open and receptive to suggestions, so they can make positive changes in their life.

During a traditional hypnosis session, the individual is typically seated or lying down in a comfortable environment. The hypnotist will use a series of techniques, such as eye fixation or guided relaxation, to help the individual enter a hypnotic state. Once the individual is in a hypnotic state, the hypnotist will deliver direct suggestions to the individual to achieve the desired outcomes. Direct suggestions may include commands such as "You will feel calm and relaxed" or "You will no longer feel the urge to smoke."

Traditional hypnosis can be effective for a variety of issues, such as smoking cessation, weight loss, and stress reduction. However, its effectiveness depends largely on the skill and experience of the hypnotist, as well as the willingness of the individual to accept and act on the suggestions. A skilled the hypnotist can tailor the suggestions to the individual's specific needs and goals, which can improve the chances of success.

One potential downside of traditional hypnosis is that it may be less effective for individuals who are highly analytical or have a strong sense of autonomy. These individuals may be resistant to direct suggestions or may not feel comfortable giving up control to the hypnotist. Traditional hypnosis may also not be suitable for individuals with certain mental health conditions, such as psychosis or severe anxiety.

Overall, traditional hypnosis remains a popular and effective method of hypnosis, particularly for individuals who are highly suggestible and comfortable with the idea of giving up control to the hypnotist. It is important to work with a qualified and experienced hypnotist to ensure the best possible outcome.

- ***Ericksonian Hypnosis***

Ericksonian hypnosis, also known as "conversational" or "indirect" hypnosis, is a method of hypnosis developed by psychiatrist and hypnotherapist Milton H. Erickson. Unlike traditional hypnosis, which relies on direct suggestions and commands to induce a trance state, Ericksonian hypnosis uses a more subtle and flexible approach.

In Ericksonian hypnosis, the hypnotist uses language and storytelling to indirectly suggest changes to the individual's thoughts, feelings, or behaviors. Instead of using direct commands or suggestions, the hypnotist uses a conversational tone and often tells stories or metaphors that are relevant to the individual's situation. These stories may be designed to help the individual see things from a new perspective or to reframe negative thoughts or experiences in a more positive light.

Ericksonian hypnosis is often used to help individuals overcome negative habits or patterns of behavior, such as smoking or overeating, as well as to reduce stress and anxiety. It can also be effective for individuals who are highly analytical or have a strong sense of autonomy, as it allows them to maintain a sense of control while still being open to suggestions.

One of the key principles of Ericksonian hypnosis is the use of "trance phenomena," which are subtle changes in the individual's behavior or physiology that indicate they are in a hypnotic state. These may include changes in breathing, eye movements, or muscle tension, as well as changes in the individual's level of suggestibility.

Another key feature of Ericksonian hypnosis is the use of "embedded commands," which are words or phrases that are embedded within a larger sentence or story. These commands may be indirect or subtle, but they are designed to plant suggestions in the individual's subconscious mind. For example, a hypnotist might tell a story about a butterfly emerging from a cocoon, with the embedded command "emerge from your old habits and behaviors."

Ericksonian hypnosis can be highly effective for a variety of issues, including anxiety, depression, phobias, and addiction. It can also be used to enhance creativity, improve self-esteem, and increase motivation. However, it requires a high level of skill and experience on the part of the hypnotist to be effective, as well as a willingness on the part of the individual to engage in the process.

Overall, Ericksonian hypnosis is a powerful and flexible method of hypnosis that can be tailored to the individual's specific needs and goals. It is particularly useful for individuals who may be resistant to direct suggestion or who prefer a more subtle approach to hypnosis. By using language and storytelling to bypass the conscious mind and access the subconscious, Ericksonian hypnosis can help individuals achieve profound and lasting change.

• *Neuro-Linguistic Programming (NLP)*

Neuro-Linguistic Programming (NLP) is a method of hypnosis that combines the principles of neuroscience, linguistics, and psychology to help individuals make positive changes in their thoughts, behaviors, and emotions. It was first developed in the 1970s by Richard Bandler and John Grinder, who studied the communication and behavioral patterns of successful therapists and communicators.

NLP is based on the idea that the way we experience the world is shaped by the language we use and the patterns of behavior we develop. By changing our language and patterns of behavior, we can change the way we think and feel about the world, and ultimately, our experience of it.

In NLP, the hypnotist uses a range of techniques to help the individual enter a hypnotic state and make positive changes. These techniques may include guided meditations, visualizations, and exercises that are designed to help the individual access their unconscious mind and create positive changes.

One of the key principles of NLP is the concept of "mapping across," which involves transferring a positive state or behavior from one context to another. For example, if an individual experiences confidence and relaxation in a particular context, such as playing a musical instrument, the hypnotist can help them transfer that state to other areas of their life where they may experience anxiety or self-doubt.

Another important principle of NLP is the use of "metaphor," which involves using stories and analogies to help the individual make positive changes. Metaphors can be used to reframe negative experiences in a more positive light or to help the individual understand complex concepts more intuitively.

NLP also incorporates the idea of "submodalities," which are the sensory details that make up our experience of the world. By changing the submodalities associated with a particular memory or experience, the individual can change their emotional response and behavior in similar situations in the future.

Overall, NLP is a powerful and effective method of hypnosis that can be used to help individuals overcome a wide range of challenges and achieve their goals. However, it requires a high level of skill and training on the part of the hypnotist, as well as a willingness on the part of the individual to engage in the process and make positive changes.

- ***Self-hypnosis***

Self-hypnosis is a method of hypnosis that involves inducing a hypnotic state in oneself, without the need for a professional hypnotist. Self-hypnosis is a technique that can be used to make positive changes to one's thoughts, behaviors, and emotions, and can be an effective tool for improving one's quality of life.

The practice of self-hypnosis involves several different techniques and strategies. For example, individuals may use relaxation techniques, such as deep breathing, to help them enter a state of relaxation and calmness. Other individuals may use visualization techniques, in which they mentally picture themselves in a situation that they find calming or empowering.

Positive affirmations are another technique that is commonly used in self-hypnosis. This involves repeating positive statements to oneself, such as "I am calm and relaxed" or "I am confident and capable." The goal of these affirmations is to help an individual develop a more positive mindset and overcome negative self-talk.

Self-hypnosis can be used to address a wide range of issues, such as anxiety, stress, phobias, and chronic pain. It can also be used to improve motivation, focus, and performance, and can be an effective tool for personal growth and development.

One of the benefits of self-hypnosis is that it can be practiced at any time, in any place. It can be used in the privacy of one's home, or during a break at work, making it a convenient and accessible tool for self-improvement.

However, it's important to note that self-hypnosis requires practice and dedication to be effective. Individuals who are new to self-hypnosis may find it challenging to enter a hypnotic state at first, and may need to experiment with different techniques and strategies to find what works best for them.

Overall, self-hypnosis is a powerful tool for personal growth and development and can be a valuable addition to an individual's self-care routine. However, it's important to approach self-hypnosis with an open mind and to seek guidance from a qualified professional if there are any concerns or questions.

• *Hypnotherapy*

Hypnotherapy is a type of complementary therapy that involves the use of hypnosis to facilitate changes in an individual's thoughts, feelings, and behaviors. Hypnosis is a natural state of heightened awareness and focus that is characterized by deep relaxation and concentration. During hypnotherapy, a trained and licensed hypnotherapist uses a variety of techniques to guide an individual into a hypnotic state, where they are more receptive to positive suggestions and can access their unconscious mind.

The hypnotherapist works with the individual to identify their goals and concerns and then suggests positive changes to their thoughts, feelings, and behaviors. For example, a hypnotherapist may use positive affirmations, guided visualizations, and other techniques to help an individual overcome negative thought patterns or behaviors, such as anxiety, depression, or addiction. Hypnotherapy can also be used to help individuals achieve goals related to personal or professional development, such as improving self-confidence, motivation, or performance.

Hypnotherapy sessions typically last between 60 and 90 minutes, and the number of sessions required will depend on the individual's goals and needs. The hypnotherapist may also provide the individual with self-hypnosis techniques and other strategies to continue working towards their goals outside of the therapy sessions.

Hypnotherapy can be used as a standalone therapy, or in conjunction with other forms of therapy, such as cognitive-behavioral therapy (CBT) or psychotherapy. It can also be used to complement medical treatments for conditions such as chronic pain, irritable bowel syndrome, and other health issues.

While hypnotherapy is generally considered safe, individuals need to work with a licensed and experienced hypnotherapist who can provide guidance and support throughout the process. Hypnotherapy is not recommended for individuals with certain medical or mental health conditions, such as epilepsy or severe mental illness, without consultation with a healthcare provider. Overall, hypnotherapy can be a highly effective form of therapy for individuals seeking to make positive changes in their thoughts, feelings, and behaviors.

The effectiveness of these methods can depend on a variety of factors, including the individual's susceptibility to hypnosis, the skill and experience of the hypnotist, and the individual's motivation to achieve their goals. It is important for individuals to do their research and choose a method that they feel comfortable with and confident in, and to work with a qualified and experienced hypnotist or therapist.

4.3 Importance of Language and Suggestion in Hypnosis

Hypnosis is a fascinating phenomenon that has been used for centuries to help individuals make positive changes in their lives. At its core, hypnosis involves inducing a state of deep relaxation and focused attention, during which the individual becomes more receptive to suggestions and can make changes to their thoughts, feelings, and behaviors.

One of the key factors in the effectiveness of hypnosis is the power of language and suggestion. The hypnotist uses language in a particular way to create a state of heightened suggestibility in the individual, allowing them to access their unconscious mind and make positive changes.

In hypnosis, the hypnotist may use a variety of language techniques to guide the individual into a hypnotic state and make positive suggestions. These techniques may include:

- ### Embedded Commands

Embedded commands are a language technique used in hypnosis to communicate positive suggestions to the unconscious mind of the individual. Embedded commands are statements that contain a direct instruction or command within the context of a larger statement, in a way that the conscious mind is not aware of the instruction, but the unconscious mind can pick up on it and respond accordingly.

In hypnosis, the use of embedded commands can be highly effective because the unconscious mind is highly receptive to indirect suggestions, and the conscious mind is often bypassed during the process. By embedding a command within a larger statement, the hypnotist can communicate a suggestion to the individual's unconscious mind, without the individual being aware of it.

For example, a hypnotist might say, "As you sit there, feeling more and more relaxed, you may find that your subconscious mind is starting to make positive changes for you." In this statement, the command "make positive changes for you" is embedded within the larger statement, and the individual's unconscious mind can receive the command without the conscious mind noticing it.

The use of embedded commands is just one of the many language techniques used in hypnosis to communicate positive suggestions to the unconscious mind of the individual. Hypnotists may also use metaphors, positive affirmations, future pacing, and other language techniques to communicate suggestions to the unconscious mind, depending on the individual's goals and needs.

It's important to note that the effectiveness of embedded commands and other language techniques in hypnosis depends on the individual's level of suggestibility, the skill and experience of the hypnotist, and the nature of the issue being addressed. Hypnosis is generally considered safe when practiced by a qualified professional, but individuals need to work with a licensed and experienced hypnotherapist to ensure their safety and well-being.

- ***Metaphors and Stories***

Metaphors and stories are powerful tools used in hypnosis to communicate with the unconscious mind of the individual. The unconscious mind is responsible for the control of many of our automatic behaviors and responses, and it is also part of the mind where emotions and memories are stored. Metaphors and stories are effective in hypnosis because they work at an unconscious level, bypassing the critical, analytical part of the mind, and allowing for direct communication with the unconscious mind.

When a hypnotist uses metaphors and stories, they are creating a situation where the individual can relate their experiences or issues to the metaphor or story being told. For example, a hypnotist might tell a story about a seed growing into a plant, which can be used as a metaphor for the individual's personal growth and development. The story can help the individual understand that just as the seed needs certain conditions to grow, they too need certain conditions to achieve their goals.

Metaphors and stories can also be used to help the individual overcome emotional or psychological blocks. For example, a hypnotist might tell a story about a bird flying free and feeling light and unburdened, to help the individual overcome feelings of heaviness or being stuck. The story can help individuals visualize themselves in a positive, empowered state, which can help them overcome negative feelings or behaviors.

The use of metaphors and stories in hypnosis is often combined with other techniques such as relaxation and suggestion. The hypnotist may use a story to help the individual relax, by painting a picture in their mind that is calming and peaceful. Once the individual is in a relaxed state, the hypnotist may then suggest positive changes to the individual's thoughts, feelings, and behaviors.

Overall, metaphors and stories are powerful tools in hypnosis because they allow for direct communication with the unconscious mind, which is often responsible for controlling many of our behaviors and responses. By using metaphors and stories, the hypnotist can help the individual relate their experiences or issues to the story being told, and in doing so, help them make positive changes to their thoughts, feelings, and behaviors.

- ### *Positive Affirmations*

Positive affirmations are a key component of hypnosis, as they are designed to help individuals change their beliefs and attitudes about themselves and their abilities. Affirmations are statements that are made in the present tense, using positive language to describe a desired outcome. In hypnosis, affirmations are used to bypass the conscious mind and speak directly to the unconscious mind, which is more receptive to positive suggestions.

Positive affirmations can be used to address a wide range of issues, from increasing self-esteem and confidence to reducing anxiety and stress. The affirmations used in hypnosis are customized to the individual's specific goals and concerns and are designed to help them make positive changes to their thoughts, feelings, and behaviors.

For example, a hypnotist might use the following affirmations to help an individual overcome a fear of flying:

1. "I am calm and relaxed when I fly"
2. "I trust the pilots and the crew to keep me safe"
3. "I enjoy traveling to new places and exploring the world"

These affirmations are repeated to the individual while they are in a hypnotic state, allowing them to become more deeply embedded in the unconscious mind. Over time, these positive affirmations can help to shift the individual's beliefs and attitudes about flying, making it easier for them to face their fear and take positive action.

It's important to note that positive affirmations alone are not enough to bring about lasting change and that hypnosis is most effective when used in conjunction with other forms of therapy or self-improvement practices. However, positive affirmations can be a powerful tool in helping individuals make positive changes to their thoughts, feelings, and behaviors, and in achieving their goals.

- ***Future Pacing***

Future pacing is a technique used in hypnosis to help individuals create a positive image of their future self, and can be an effective tool for achieving goals and overcoming challenges. The technique involves guiding the individual into a relaxed state of hypnosis and then using language to help them imagine and visualize themselves in a positive future state.

In future pacing, the hypnotist will typically use language that creates a vivid and detailed picture of the individual's desired future state. This may include descriptions of what the individual will see, hear, and feel when they have achieved their goal or overcome their challenge.

For example, if an individual is seeking to overcome a fear of public speaking, the hypnotist may guide them into a state of hypnosis and then use language to help them imagine themselves giving a successful and confident speech to a large audience. The hypnotist may describe the setting, the emotions the individual is feeling, and the positive reactions of the audience.

The idea behind future pacing is that by visualizing and experiencing a positive future state in hypnosis, the individual is more likely to be able to achieve that state in real life. The technique helps to build confidence and motivation and provides a clear and compelling image of what the individual is working towards.

It's important to note that while future pacing can be a powerful tool for achieving goals and overcoming challenges, it is not a magic solution. The effectiveness of future pacings, like any hypnosis technique, will depend on a variety of factors, including the individual's willingness to engage in the process, the skill and experience of the hypnotist, and the nature of the issue being addressed.

In summary, future pacing is a technique used in hypnosis to help individuals create a positive image of their future selves. By guiding the individual into a state of deep relaxation and using language to create a vivid and detailed picture of a positive future state, future pacing can be an effective tool for achieving goals and overcoming challenges.

The power of language and suggestion in hypnosis is rooted in the fact that language can have a profound effect on the way we think, feel, and behave. In hypnosis, the individual is in a heightened state of suggestibility, making them more open to the power of language and the positive suggestions that are being made.

However, it's important to note that hypnosis is not a magic solution, and the effectiveness of hypnosis will depend on a variety of factors, including the individual's willingness to engage in the process, the skill and experience of the hypnotist, and the nature of the issue being addressed.

In conclusion, the importance of language and suggestion in hypnosis cannot be overstated. The hypnotist uses language in a particular way to create a state of heightened suggestibility in the individual, allowing them to access their unconscious mind and make positive changes. By understanding and utilizing the power of language in hypnosis, individuals can make positive changes to their thoughts, feelings, and behaviors, and achieve their goals.

The Benefits of Hypnosis

Overview

- ❖ **The Benefits of Hypnosis**

  - ✓ *Stress Management*
  - ✓ *Better Sleep*
  - ✓ *Pain Management*
  - ✓ *Weight Loss*
  - ✓ *Controlled Drugs Addiction*
  - ✓ *Minimizes Anxiety and Depression*
  - ✓ *Boosted Self-esteem*
  - ✓ *Better Performance*
  - ✓ *Improves Memory*
  - ✓ *Raises Creativity*

- ❖ **The Potential Downsides and Risks of Hypnosis**

  - ✓ *False Memories*
  - ✓ *Increased Susceptibility to Suggestion*
  - ✓ *Unwanted Emotions or Sensations*
  - ✓ *Dependence*
  - ✓ *Lack of Regulation*

- ❖ **The Use of Hypnosis in Different Industries**

  - ✓ *Entertainment Industry*
  - ✓ *Sports Industry*
  - ✓ *Education Industry*
  - ✓ *Law Enforcement Industry*

5.1 *The Benefits of Hypnosis*

Hypnosis is a technique that has been used for centuries to treat a variety of mental and physical health issues. This therapeutic approach involves inducing a trance-like state of consciousness that can enhance an individual's responsiveness to suggestions, reduce their inhibitions, and promote relaxation. While the efficacy of hypnosis remains controversial in some circles, a growing body of research has shown that hypnosis can have a wide range of benefits. Here are some of the benefits of hypnosis:

- ### *Stress Management*

Stress is a common experience for many people in today's fast-paced, high-pressure world. While a certain amount of stress can be motivating, chronic stress can have serious negative effects on physical and mental health. Hypnosis is one technique that has been shown to help individuals manage stress more effectively.

Hypnosis involves inducing a trance-like state of consciousness that can enhance an individual's responsiveness to suggestions, reduce their inhibitions, and promote relaxation. During hypnosis, the individual is guided into a relaxed state that allows them to become more receptive to positive suggestions and imagery. The hypnotist may use a variety of techniques to promote relaxation and reduce stress, including deep breathing exercises, progressive muscle relaxation, guided imagery, and positive affirmations.

Research has shown that hypnosis can be an effective treatment for stress relief. In a study published in the Journal of Alternative and Complementary Medicine, participants who received hypnosis treatment for stress reduction reported significant improvements in their mental and physical well-being. Hypnosis has also been shown to be effective in reducing stress and anxiety related to medical procedures, such as surgery and dental work.

One of the reasons why hypnosis is effective in managing stress is that it helps individuals to access their subconscious mind. The subconscious mind is responsible for regulating many of the body's automatic functions, including heart rate, breathing, and digestion. By accessing the subconscious mind, hypnosis can help individuals to influence these automatic functions, promoting relaxation and reducing feelings of stress and anxiety.

In addition, hypnosis can be used to address underlying psychological factors that may be contributing to stress. For example, individuals may be experiencing stress due to unresolved emotional issues or negative self-talk. Hypnosis can be used to help individuals identify and address these underlying psychological factors, promoting positive self-talk and reducing negative emotions.

In conclusion, hypnosis can be an effective treatment for stress relief. By inducing a relaxed, trance-like state, hypnosis can help individuals reduce feelings of anxiety and tension. In addition, hypnosis can be used to address underlying psychological factors that may be contributing to stress, promoting positive self-talk and reducing negative emotions. Whether used as a standalone treatment or in conjunction with other therapies, hypnosis can help individuals manage stress more effectively and lead happier healthier lives.

- ***Better Sleep***

Many people struggle with getting a good night's sleep, and chronic sleep problems can have negative effects on physical and mental health. Hypnosis is one technique that has been shown to help individuals improve their sleep quality and reduce insomnia.

Hypnosis involves inducing a trance-like state of consciousness that can enhance an individual's responsiveness to suggestions, reduce their inhibitions, and promote relaxation. During hypnosis, the individual is guided into a relaxed state that allows them to become more receptive to positive suggestions and imagery. The hypnotist may use a variety of techniques to promote relaxation and reduce stress, including deep breathing exercises, progressive muscle relaxation, guided imagery, and positive affirmations.

Research has shown that hypnosis can be an effective treatment for improving sleep quality and reducing insomnia. In a study published in the Journal of Clinical Sleep Medicine, participants who received hypnosis treatment for insomnia reported significant improvements in their sleep quality and quantity. Hypnosis has also been shown to be effective in reducing sleep problems associated with medical conditions, such as chronic pain and cancer.

One of the reasons why hypnosis is effective in improving sleep is that it helps individuals to access their subconscious minds. The subconscious mind is responsible for regulating many of the body's automatic functions, including sleep. By accessing the subconscious mind, hypnosis can help individuals to influence these automatic functions, promoting relaxation and reducing sleep disturbances.

In addition, hypnosis can be used to address underlying psychological factors that may be contributing to sleep problems. For example, individuals may be experiencing sleep problems due to anxiety, stress, or negative thought patterns. Hypnosis can be used to help individuals identify and address these underlying psychological factors, promoting positive self-talk and reducing negative emotions.

Overall, hypnosis can be an effective treatment for improving sleep quality and reducing insomnia. By inducing a relaxed, trance-like state, hypnosis can help individuals promote relaxation and reduce sleep disturbances. In addition, hypnosis can be used to address underlying psychological factors that may be contributing to sleep problems, promoting positive self-talk and reducing negative emotions. Whether used as a standalone treatment or in conjunction with other therapies, hypnosis can help individuals get the good night's sleep they need to lead happier, healthier lives.

- ### *Pain Management*

Pain is a complex experience that involves both physical and psychological components. While medication and other medical treatments can be effective for managing pain, hypnosis is another technique that is effective for pain management.

Hypnosis involves inducing a trance-like state of consciousness that can enhance an individual's responsiveness to suggestions, reduce their inhibitions, and promote relaxation. During hypnosis, the individual is guided into a relaxed state that allows them to become more receptive to positive suggestions and imagery. The hypnotist may use a variety of techniques to promote relaxation and reduce stress, including deep breathing exercises, progressive muscle relaxation, guided imagery, and positive affirmations.

Research has shown that hypnosis can be an effective treatment for pain management. In a study published in the journal Pain, participants who received hypnosis treatment for chronic pain reported significant reductions in pain intensity, as well as improvements in mood, sleep, and quality of life. Hypnosis has also been shown to be effective in reducing pain related to medical procedures, such as surgery and childbirth.

One of the reasons why hypnosis is effective in managing pain is that it can help individuals to alter their perception of pain. Pain is not simply a physical sensation, but is also influenced by psychological and emotional factors. By inducing a relaxed state and promoting positive suggestions and imagery, hypnosis can help individuals to reduce their perception of pain, as well as their emotional response to pain.

In addition, hypnosis can be used to address underlying psychological factors that may be contributing to pain. For example, individuals may be experiencing pain due to anxiety, stress, or unresolved emotional issues. Hypnosis can be used to help individuals identify and address these underlying psychological factors, promoting positive self-talk and reducing negative emotions.

Overall, hypnosis can be an effective treatment for pain management. By inducing a relaxed, trance-like state, hypnosis can help individuals alter their perception of pain and reduce their emotional response to pain. In addition, hypnosis can be used to address underlying psychological factors that may be contributing to pain, promoting positive self-talk and reducing negative emotions. Whether used as a standalone treatment or in conjunction with other therapies, hypnosis can be a valuable tool for managing pain and improving quality of life.

- ### *Weight Loss*

Hypnosis has gained popularity as a tool for weight loss, with many individuals turning to hypnotherapy to help them achieve their weight loss goals. Hypnosis for weight loss involves inducing a trance-like state of consciousness that can enhance an individual's responsiveness to suggestions, reduce their inhibitions, and promote relaxation. During hypnosis, the individual is guided into a relaxed state that allows them to become more receptive to positive suggestions and imagery. The hypnotist may use a variety of techniques to promote relaxation and reduce stress, including deep breathing exercises, progressive muscle relaxation, guided imagery, and positive affirmations.

Hypnosis for weight loss typically involves changing the individual's behavior and mindset to help them adopt healthier habits and make better choices. The hypnotist may use a variety of techniques to help the individual overcome negative thought patterns, reduce emotional eating, and increase motivation for exercise and healthy eating.

Research has shown that hypnosis can be an effective treatment for weight loss. In a study published in the International Journal of Clinical and Experimental Hypnosis, participants who received hypnosis treatment for weight loss reported significant reductions in body weight, body mass index (BMI), and waist circumference. Hypnosis has also been shown to be effective in reducing binge eating and emotional eating.

One of the reasons why hypnosis is effective for weight loss is that it can help individuals to access their subconscious mind. The subconscious mind is responsible for regulating many of the body's automatic functions, including hunger and satiety. By accessing the subconscious mind, hypnosis can help individuals to influence these automatic functions, promoting healthy eating habits and reducing cravings.

In addition, hypnosis can be used to address underlying psychological factors that may be contributing to weight gain. For example, individuals may be overeating due to stress, anxiety, or unresolved emotional issues. Hypnosis can be used to help individuals identify and address these underlying psychological factors, promoting positive self-talk and reducing negative emotions.

Overall, hypnosis can be an effective tool for weight loss. By inducing a relaxed, trance-like state, hypnosis can help individuals adopt healthier habits and make better choices. In addition, hypnosis can be used to address underlying psychological factors that may be contributing to weight gain, promoting positive self-talk and reducing negative emotions. Whether used as a standalone treatment or in conjunction with other therapies, hypnosis can be a valuable tool for achieving weight loss and improving overall health.

- ### *Controlled Drugs Addiction*

The use of hypnosis as a treatment for drug addiction is a controversial and complex topic. While some research has shown that hypnosis can be an effective addiction treatment, other studies have not found significant benefits.

Hypnosis for drug addiction involves inducing a trance-like state of consciousness that can enhance an individual's responsiveness to suggestions, reduce their inhibitions, and promote relaxation. During hypnosis, the individual is guided into a relaxed state that allows them to become more receptive to positive suggestions and imagery. The hypnotist may use a variety of techniques to promote relaxation and reduce stress, including deep breathing exercises, progressive muscle relaxation, guided imagery, and positive affirmations.

One of the ways that hypnosis can be used to treat drug addiction is by addressing the underlying psychological factors that may be contributing to the addiction. For example, individuals may be using drugs to cope with anxiety, depression, or trauma. By using hypnosis to address these underlying issues, individuals may be able to reduce their reliance on drugs and find healthier coping strategies.

Another way that hypnosis can be used to treat drug addiction is by helping individuals to change their patterns of behavior and thoughts related to drug use. For example, hypnosis can be used to help individuals overcome cravings, reduce their use of drugs, and adopt healthier habits.

While some research has shown that hypnosis can be an effective treatment for drug addiction, the evidence is not conclusive. A review of the literature published in the Journal of Addictive Diseases found that while some studies have shown positive results, other studies have not found significant benefits of hypnosis for addiction.

It is also important to note that hypnosis should not be used as a standalone treatment for drug addiction. Rather, it should be used in conjunction with other evidence-based treatments, such as medication-assisted treatment, counseling, and support groups.

In summary, hypnosis can be a useful tool in the treatment of drug addiction. By inducing a relaxed, trance-like state, hypnosis can help individuals address underlying psychological factors that may be contributing to addiction, as well as change their patterns of behavior and thoughts related to drug use. However, more research is needed to fully understand the potential benefits and limitations of hypnosis for drug addiction, and it should be used in conjunction with other evidence-based treatments.

- ### *Minimizes Anxiety and Depression*

Hypnosis is a complementary therapy that can be used to help manage anxiety and depression. Hypnosis involves inducing a trance-like state of consciousness that can enhance an individual's responsiveness to suggestions, reduce their inhibitions, and promote relaxation. During hypnosis, the individual is guided into a relaxed state that allows them to become more receptive to positive suggestions and imagery. The hypnotist may use a variety of techniques to promote relaxation and reduce stress, including deep breathing exercises, progressive muscle relaxation, guided imagery, and positive affirmations.

Anxiety and depression are often linked to negative thought patterns and beliefs, such as excessive worry, self-criticism, and pessimism. Hypnosis can be used to help individuals identify and challenge these negative thoughts, promoting more positive self-talk and a more optimistic outlook on life. By reducing negative thought patterns, hypnosis can help individuals to feel more relaxed, confident, and in control.

Research has shown that hypnosis can be an effective treatment for anxiety and depression. A review of the literature published in the American Journal of Clinical Hypnosis found that hypnosis can be used to reduce anxiety symptoms, such as panic attacks, phobias, and social anxiety. In addition, hypnosis is effective in reducing symptoms of depression, such as low mood, fatigue, and hopelessness.

One of the ways that hypnosis can be used to treat anxiety and depression is by addressing the underlying psychological factors that may be contributing to these conditions. For example, individuals may be experiencing anxiety and depression due to stress, trauma, or unresolved emotional issues. By using hypnosis to address these underlying issues, individuals may be able to reduce their symptoms and find healthier coping strategies.

Another way that hypnosis can be used to treat anxiety and depression is by helping individuals to develop positive coping skills and strategies. For example, hypnosis can be used to help individuals develop relaxation techniques, such as deep breathing exercises and progressive muscle relaxation. Hypnosis can also be used to help individuals develop a more positive self-image, promoting more self-confidence and self-esteem.

Overall, hypnosis can be a useful tool in the treatment of anxiety and depression. By inducing a relaxed, trance-like state, hypnosis can help individuals identify and challenge negative thought patterns, address underlying psychological factors and develop positive coping skills and strategies. However, it should be used in conjunction with other evidence-based treatments, such as medication and psychotherapy, and under the guidance of a trained hypnotherapist.

- ### *Boosted Self-esteem*

Hypnosis is a complementary therapy that can be used to help improve self-esteem. Self-esteem refers to an individual's subjective evaluation of their worth and value. A healthy level of self-esteem is important for overall mental health and well-being, as it can impact how individuals feel about themselves, how they interact with others, and how they approach new challenges.

Hypnosis can be used to help individuals develop a more positive self-image and promote greater self-esteem. During hypnosis, the individual is guided into a relaxed state that allows them to become more receptive to positive suggestions and imagery. The hypnotist may use a variety of techniques to promote relaxation and reduce stress, including deep breathing exercises, progressive muscle relaxation, guided imagery, and positive affirmations.

One of the ways that hypnosis can be used to improve self-esteem is by helping individuals to identify and challenge negative self-talk. Negative self-talk can contribute to feelings of low self-worth and may be a result of past negative experiences, unrealistic expectations, or anxiety. By using hypnosis to identify and challenge negative self-talk, individuals can develop more positive and realistic thoughts about themselves and their abilities.

Another way that hypnosis can be used to improve self-esteem is by helping individuals to develop a more positive self-image. Hypnosis can be used to promote positive self-talk, visualization, and affirmations. For example, the hypnotist may guide the individual through a visualization exercise in which they imagine themselves achieving their goals or being confident in a particular situation. By practicing positive self-talk and visualization, individuals can develop a more positive self-image and greater self-esteem.

Research has shown that hypnosis can be an effective treatment for improving self-esteem. A review of the literature published in the American Journal of Clinical Hypnosis found that hypnosis can be used to promote positive self-talk, reduce negative self-talk, and promote self-confidence.

Overall, hypnosis can be a useful tool in improving self-esteem. By inducing a relaxed, trance-like state, hypnosis can help individuals identify and challenge negative self-talk, develop a more positive self-image, and promote greater self-esteem. However, it should be used in conjunction with other evidence-based treatments, such as cognitive-behavioral therapy, and under the guidance of a trained hypnotherapist.

- ### *Better Performance*

Hypnosis has been used to enhance performance in a wide range of areas, including sports, public speaking, creative arts, and academic pursuits. Performance anxiety can be a significant barrier to achieving one's goals, and hypnosis can be used to alleviate these anxieties and improve performance outcomes.

One of the ways that hypnosis can enhance performance is by promoting a state of deep relaxation. When the body is relaxed, the mind is more focused and alert, and the individual is better able to concentrate on the task at hand. By guiding the individual into a relaxed state, the hypnotist can help them to overcome distractions and stay focused on their performance.

Another way that hypnosis can enhance performance is by improving self-confidence. When individuals are confident in their abilities, they are more likely to perform well under pressure. Hypnosis can be used to promote positive self-talk and visualization, which can help individuals to develop greater confidence in their abilities.

Hypnosis can also be used to help individuals overcome performance anxiety. Performance anxiety can manifest as physical symptoms such as sweating, shaking, and rapid heartbeat. By using hypnosis to address the root causes of performance anxiety, individuals can develop coping strategies to manage these symptoms and perform at their best.

Research has shown that hypnosis can be an effective tool for enhancing performance. A review of the literature published in the International Journal of Clinical and Experimental Hypnosis found that hypnosis can be used to improve athletic performance, academic performance, and public speaking skills.

In conclusion, hypnosis can be a useful tool for enhancing performance in a wide range of areas. By promoting relaxation, improving self-confidence, and helping individuals to manage performance anxiety, hypnosis can help individuals to overcome barriers to success and achieve their goals. However, it is important to note that hypnosis should be used in conjunction with other evidence-based treatments and under the guidance of a trained hypnotherapist.

- ***Improves Memory***

Hypnosis can be used to improve memory performance in a variety of settings, such as academic studies, job training, and personal life. Memory is a complex cognitive process that involves encoding, storage, and retrieval of information, and hypnosis can help individuals to enhance each of these aspects.

One way that hypnosis can improve memory performance is by enhancing the encoding of information. During hypnosis, individuals are guided into a relaxed state that makes them more receptive to suggestions and imagery. By using hypnosis to promote a state of focused attention, the hypnotist can help the individual to improve the encoding of information, making it easier to remember later.

Another way that hypnosis can improve memory performance is by promoting the use of mental imagery. Hypnosis can be used to help individuals create vivid mental images of information they wish to remember, such as important dates, phone numbers, or names. By associating this information with mental images, individuals are more likely to remember it later.

Hypnosis can also be used to improve memory retrieval. During hypnosis, the hypnotist can guide the individual to access memories that may be difficult to recall. Hypnosis can also be used to help individuals to overcome mental blocks or negative associations that may be interfering with memory retrieval.

Research has shown that hypnosis can be an effective tool for improving memory performance. A review of the literature published in the International Journal of Clinical and Experimental Hypnosis found that hypnosis can be used to enhance memory performance in a variety of contexts, including academic studies, job training, and personal life.

In conclusion, hypnosis can be a useful tool for improving memory performance. By enhancing encoding, promoting mental imagery, and improving memory retrieval, hypnosis can help individuals to better remember information and perform more effectively in academic, professional, and personal settings. However, it is important to note that hypnosis should be used in conjunction with other evidence-based treatments and under the guidance of a trained hypnotherapist.

- ***Raises Creativity***

Hypnosis can be a useful tool for enhancing creativity in a variety of fields, including the arts, writing, and problem-solving. Creativity involves the ability to generate new ideas and approaches, and hypnosis can be used to stimulate this process by promoting a state of relaxed, focused attention and by accessing the subconscious mind.

One way that hypnosis can enhance creativity is by promoting a state of relaxation. When individuals are relaxed, they are more open to new ideas and better able to think creatively. By guiding individuals into a state of deep relaxation, hypnosis can help them to access their inner creativity and generate new ideas.

Hypnosis can also be used to access the subconscious mind, which is thought to be a rich source of creative inspiration. By accessing the subconscious mind through hypnosis, individuals can tap into their inner creativity and generate new ideas and approaches.

Another way that hypnosis can enhance creativity is by promoting mental flexibility. Hypnosis can be used to help individuals overcome mental blocks and negative self-talk that may be hindering their creative process. By promoting mental flexibility, hypnosis can help individuals to approach problems from new angles and generate novel solutions.

Research has shown that hypnosis can be an effective tool for enhancing creativity. A study published in The Journal of Creative Behavior found that individuals who underwent a hypnosis session reported increased levels of creativity compared to those who did not receive hypnosis.

In conclusion, hypnosis can be a useful tool for enhancing creativity. By promoting relaxation, accessing the subconscious mind, and promoting mental flexibility, hypnosis can help individuals to tap into their inner creativity and generate new ideas and approaches. However, it is important to note that hypnosis should be used in conjunction with other evidence-based treatments and under the guidance of a trained hypnotherapist.

In summary, hypnosis can have a wide range of benefits for individuals seeking to improve their physical and mental well-being. Whether used as a standalone treatment or in conjunction with other therapies, hypnosis can help many people lead happier, healthier lives.

5.2 The Potential Downsides and Risks of Hypnosis

While hypnosis is generally considered safe when used by a trained and licensed practitioner, there are some potential downsides and risks that individuals should be aware of:

- ### *False Memories*

One of the potential risks of hypnosis is the formation of false memories. False memories are memories of events or experiences that never actually occurred, but which are believed to be true by the individual who has the memory. In hypnosis, individuals may be more susceptible to suggestions and may be more likely to create or accept false memories.

There are a few ways that false memories can occur in hypnosis. First, the hypnotherapist may unintentionally suggest or prompt the individual to recall information or events that they have not experienced. For example, the hypnotherapist may ask leading questions or make statements that suggest a particular event or experience occurred, even if it did not. This can lead the individual to incorporate these suggestions into their memories and believe that they are true.

Second, false memories can also occur when the individual is actively trying to recall past events or experiences. In hypnosis, the individual may be in a highly suggestible state and may be more likely to create or accept false memories as a way of filling in gaps or uncertainties in their memories.

There are several risks associated with false memories in hypnosis. For example, false memories can have serious consequences in legal or therapeutic settings. In legal cases, false memories can lead to wrongful convictions or false accusations, while in therapeutic settings, false memories can lead to misdiagnosis or inappropriate treatment.

To minimize the risk of false memories in hypnosis, it is important to work with a trained and licensed hypnotherapist who adheres to ethical and professional standards. Hypnotherapists should avoid leading questions or statements that suggest a particular event or experience occurred and should encourage individuals to rely on their memories and experiences rather than accepting suggestions or prompts.

In conclusion, false memories can be a potential risk of hypnosis, particularly if the hypnotherapist is not trained to avoid leading questions or suggestions. However, with proper training and ethical practices, hypnosis can be a safe and effective treatment for a variety of conditions.

- ### *Increased Susceptibility to Suggestion*

Hypnosis involves inducing a trance-like state in which an individual becomes highly focused, relaxed, and receptive to suggestion. During this state, the individual may be more susceptible to suggestions and may be more likely to accept and act on suggestions made by the hypnotherapist or others.

This increased susceptibility to suggestion can have both positive and negative consequences. On the one hand, it can make hypnosis a highly effective tool for behavior modification and self-improvement. For example, suggestions made during hypnosis can help individuals to overcome negative thought patterns, improve self-esteem, and develop new habits and behaviors.

On the other hand, this increased susceptibility to suggestion can also be a potential risk of hypnosis. For example, the individual may be more likely to accept and act on suggestions that are unethical or harmful, or that conflict with their values and beliefs. In some cases, this can lead to inappropriate or even dangerous behaviors.

Several factors can affect an individual's susceptibility to suggestion during hypnosis. For example, some individuals may be more suggestible than others due to their personality, beliefs, or past experiences. Additionally, the effectiveness of hypnosis can be influenced by the skill and experience of the hypnotherapist, as well as the quality and content of the suggestions being made.

To minimize the risk of negative outcomes related to increased susceptibility to suggestion, it is important to work with a qualified and experienced hypnotherapist who follows ethical and professional standards. The hypnotherapist should avoid making suggestions that conflict with the individual's values and beliefs, and should encourage the individual to maintain a sense of control and agency during the hypnosis session.

In conclusion, increased susceptibility to suggestion is a potential risk of hypnosis, but with proper training and ethical practices, it can be a highly effective tool for behavior modification and self-improvement. It is important to work with a qualified and experienced hypnotherapist to ensure that the hypnosis session is safe, effective, and aligned with the individual's goals and values.

- ***Unwanted Emotions or Sensations***

Hypnosis involves inducing a state of focused attention and relaxation in which an individual is more receptive to suggestions made by a hypnotherapist. While this state of heightened suggestibility can be beneficial for achieving desired changes in behavior or mindset, it can also lead to unwanted emotions or sensations.

During hypnosis, individuals may experience a range of emotional or physical sensations, including relaxation, warmth, tingling, or heaviness. In some cases, individuals may also experience unexpected or unwanted emotions, such as anxiety, fear, or sadness. These sensations and emotions may be the result of the individual's unconscious mind bringing forward repressed memories or emotions, or they may be a response to the suggestions made by the hypnotherapist.

While the sensations and emotions experienced during hypnosis can be uncomfortable or distressing, they are generally not harmful and will typically fade once the hypnosis session is over. However, in rare cases, individuals may experience more significant or persistent emotional or physical symptoms as a result of hypnosis.

It is important for individuals considering hypnosis to discuss any concerns they have with their hypnotherapist and to work together to establish a safe and comfortable environment for the hypnosis session. The hypnotherapist should be trained and experienced in working with individuals who may experience unexpected or unwanted emotions or sensations during hypnosis and should be able to provide guidance and support throughout the session.

In conclusion, unwanted emotions or sensations are a potential risk of hypnosis, but they are generally not harmful and will typically fade once the hypnosis session is over. It is important for individuals considering hypnosis to discuss any concerns they have with their hypnotherapist and to work together to establish a safe and comfortable environment for the hypnosis session. With proper guidance and support, hypnosis can be a highly effective tool for behavior modification, self-improvement, and emotional healing.

- ### *Dependence*

One potential risk associated with hypnosis is the possibility of dependence on the hypnotic state. Dependence on hypnosis can occur when an individual becomes reliant on the hypnotic state to manage their emotions or cope with stressful situations. This can be particularly problematic if the individual is using hypnosis to avoid dealing with underlying issues or if they are using hypnosis as a substitute for traditional mental health treatment.

Individuals who become dependent on hypnosis may experience negative consequences when they are unable to access the hypnotic state. They may experience increased anxiety or stress or may find it difficult to manage their emotions without the support of hypnosis. This can also lead to a cycle of dependence, where the individual becomes more reliant on hypnosis to manage their emotions, and may be less likely to seek out other forms of treatment.

One factor that can contribute to dependence on hypnosis is the nature of the hypnotic state itself. Hypnosis can be a deeply relaxing and trance-like state, and individuals may find it to be a welcome escape from stress or anxiety. However, it is important to remember that hypnosis is a tool for managing specific symptoms or behaviors, and should not be relied on as the sole method for managing one's mental health.

Another factor that can contribute to dependence on hypnosis is how hypnosis is used. If an individual is using hypnosis to avoid dealing with underlying issues, or if they are using hypnosis as a substitute for traditional mental health treatment, they may be more likely to become dependent on the hypnotic state. Individuals need to work with a qualified hypnotherapist who can help them use hypnosis in a way that is safe and effective.

It is also important for individuals to be aware that hypnosis is not a replacement for traditional mental health treatment. While hypnosis can be a powerful tool for managing specific symptoms or behaviors, it should be used as part of a comprehensive treatment plan that includes other forms of therapy, medication, and support.

In conclusion, dependence on hypnosis is a potential risk associated with the use of hypnosis. Individuals who become dependent on hypnosis may experience negative consequences when they are unable to access the hypnotic state and may be less likely to seek out other forms of treatment. It is important for individuals to work with a qualified hypnotherapist, and to use hypnosis as part of a comprehensive treatment plan that includes other forms of therapy and support.

- ***Lack of Regulation***

Another potential risk associated with hypnosis is the lack of regulation in the field. Unlike many other forms of mental health treatment, hypnotherapy is not a licensed or regulated profession in many countries, including the United States. This means that anyone can call themselves a hypnotherapist and offer hypnosis services, regardless of their level of training or experience.

The lack of regulation in the field can make it difficult for individuals to find a qualified and experienced hypnotherapist. This can be particularly problematic for individuals who are seeking hypnosis as a treatment for a mental health condition, as they may be vulnerable to unethical or ineffective practices.

In addition to the lack of regulation in the field, there is also a lack of standardized training and certification requirements for hypnotherapists. While there are many training programs available for hypnotherapists, the quality and rigor of these programs can vary widely. This can make it difficult for individuals to assess the credentials and qualifications of a hypnotherapist.

Another potential risk associated with the lack of regulation in the field is the potential for hypnotherapists to make unfounded or unsupported claims about the efficacy of hypnosis. While there is evidence to support the use of hypnosis for certain conditions, there are also many claims made about the benefits of hypnosis that are not supported by scientific research.

It is important for individuals to do their research and carefully vet potential hypnotherapists before working with them. This may involve asking for recommendations from trusted healthcare professionals or seeking out hypnotherapists who are members of professional organizations, such as the

American Society of Clinical Hypnosis. It is also important for individuals to be aware of the limitations of hypnosis as a treatment, and to work with a hypnotherapist who is transparent about the risks and benefits of hypnosis.

In conclusion, the lack of regulation in the field of hypnotherapy is a potential risk associated with the use of hypnosis. This can make it difficult for individuals to find qualified and experienced hypnotherapists and may leave them vulnerable to unethical or ineffective practices. It is important for individuals to carefully vet potential hypnotherapists, and to work with a hypnotherapist who is transparent about the risks and benefits of hypnosis.

It is important to note that these risks and downsides are not common and can be minimized by working with a trained and licensed hypnotherapist who adheres to ethical and professional standards. It is also important to talk to a healthcare provider before using hypnosis as a treatment for any condition, particularly if you have an underlying medical or mental health condition.

5.3 *The Use of Hypnosis in Different Industries*

Hypnosis, a state of heightened suggestibility and deep relaxation, has been used in various industries for many years. It is perhaps most commonly associated with mental health and therapy, but it has a wide range of applications in other fields as well. Let's explore the use of hypnosis in different industries, including entertainment, sports, education, and law enforcement.

- ### *Entertainment Industry*

The entertainment industry is one of the sectors where hypnosis has been widely used. Hypnosis shows, also known as hypnosis entertainment, have become increasingly popular over the years, with performers like Derren Brown, Paul McKenna, and others who have used hypnosis to entertain audiences.

In hypnosis entertainment, a trained hypnotherapist or entertainer puts volunteers into a trance-like state and then gives them suggestions or commands. The volunteers then perform various activities, such as dancing, singing, or acting in a way that the hypnotist suggests. These activities are often amusing and entertaining for the audience.

Hypnosis entertainment has been a source of controversy, with some critics arguing that it can be exploitative or unethical. For example, some argue that the hypnotist can use their power to embarrass or humiliate volunteers, or that the volunteers might not fully understand what they are agreeing to when they volunteer. It is therefore important for hypnosis entertainers to be trained in ethical and responsible hypnosis practices.

On the other hand, supporters of hypnosis entertainment argue that it can be a fun and enjoyable experience for both the volunteers and the audience. They also argue that it can help to break down social barriers and encourage people to let go of their inhibitions.

Overall, the use of hypnosis in the entertainment industry has become a popular way of providing entertainment, but hypnotherapists and performers need to use their skills responsibly and ethically.

- ***Sports Industry***

The sports industry is another sector where hypnosis has been used to improve performance. Athletes have long sought ways to improve their mental and physical abilities, and hypnosis is one technique that has been used to help them achieve their goals.

One of the main ways hypnosis is used in the sports industry is to help athletes overcome mental barriers, such as anxiety, self-doubt, and fear of failure. These barriers can be just as detrimental to an athlete's performance as physical injuries, and hypnosis can be used to help them overcome these challenges.

Hypnosis can also be used to help athletes improve their physical abilities. For example, a hypnotist can use suggestion and visualization techniques to help an athlete improve their coordination, endurance, and overall physical performance. By visualizing themselves as succeeding in their sport, athletes can gain a mental edge that can help them perform at a higher level.

In addition, hypnosis can be used to help athletes recover from injuries. By using hypnosis to reduce pain and promote healing, athletes can recover more quickly from injuries and get back to training and competing sooner.

Overall, the use of hypnosis in the sports industry has become an increasingly popular way of helping athletes improve their performance. While the effectiveness of hypnosis is still up for debate, many athletes and coaches have reported positive results from using hypnosis as part of their training and performance-enhancement techniques.

- ***Education Industry***

Hypnosis has been used in the education industry to help students overcome various academic and personal challenges. Hypnosis is typically used as a complementary approach to traditional teaching methods, and it is often used in combination with other techniques, such as cognitive-behavioral therapy.

One of the primary uses of hypnosis in the education industry is to help students improve their study habits and academic performance. Hypnosis can be used to help students overcome test anxiety, improve memory retention, and increase motivation to study. By using suggestion and visualization techniques, hypnosis can help students develop positive attitudes toward learning and increase their confidence in their academic abilities.

Hypnosis can also be used to help students overcome personal challenges that may be impacting their academic performance. For example, hypnosis can be used to help students overcome stress, anxiety, depression, and other emotional issues that may be impacting their ability to learn. By addressing these underlying issues, hypnosis can help students improve their overall well-being and academic performance.

Another use of hypnosis in the education industry is to help students with learning disabilities, such as dyslexia and ADHD. Hypnosis can be used to help these students improve their focus, concentration, and cognitive abilities. By addressing the underlying neurological and psychological factors that are contributing to these disabilities, hypnosis can help students improve their overall academic performance.

Overall, hypnosis can be a useful tool in the education industry, helping students to overcome academic and personal challenges and improve their overall academic performance. While the use of hypnosis in the education industry is not yet widely accepted, many educators and researchers are exploring the potential benefits of this approach and exploring new ways to incorporate hypnosis into the classroom.

- ***Law Enforcement Industry***

The use of hypnosis in law enforcement has been a controversial topic for several decades. The practice of hypnosis in this industry is used as a tool to help witnesses and victims recall details of a crime or event that may have been forgotten or repressed in their memory.

Law enforcement agencies have used hypnosis to assist in the investigation of various crimes, including homicides, sexual assaults, and robberies. Hypnosis is used as an investigative tool to enhance the memory recall of victims or witnesses, allowing them to provide more detailed and accurate descriptions of events and suspects.

However, the use of hypnosis in law enforcement is not without controversy. One concern is the potential for suggestibility and false memories. When a person is hypnotized, they become more suggestible, which means they may be more likely to provide false information, or they may remember details that did not occur.

The use of hypnosis in law enforcement is also not regulated in the same way that other investigative techniques, such as DNA testing or fingerprint analysis, are. This lack of regulation can lead to the potential misuse of hypnosis or even abuse by law enforcement officials.

Despite the potential risks, hypnosis can be a valuable tool in certain situations. It is important to ensure that the hypnosis is conducted by a trained and licensed professional and that proper safeguards are put in place to prevent the risk of false memories.

In recent years, some law enforcement agencies have shifted away from using hypnosis as an investigative tool due to concerns about its reliability and validity. However, some agencies still use hypnosis in certain cases, particularly when traditional investigative methods have been exhausted or have not yielded sufficient results.

Overall, hypnosis has a wide range of applications and can be used in many different industries. While it is perhaps most commonly associated with mental health and therapy, it has proven to be a useful tool in entertainment, sports, education, and law enforcement. It is important to note, however, that the effectiveness of hypnosis can vary from person to person, and it should always be used ethically and responsibly.

Overcoming Fears and Skepticism

Overview

❖ **Common Misconceptions and Fears about Hypnosis**

  ✓ *Hypnosis is Mind Control*
  ✓ *Hypnosis is a Magical or Mystical Practice*
  ✓ *Only Weak-minded People can be Hypnotized*
  ✓ *Hypnosis can Erase Memories or Create False Memories*
  ✓ *Hypnosis is Dangerous*

❖ **The Ethical Considerations and Guidelines**

  ✓ *Informed Consent*
  ✓ *Professional Boundaries*
  ✓ *Competence*
  ✓ *Avoiding Harm*
  ✓ *Cultural Sensitivity*

❖ **The Scientific Evidence Supporting the Effectiveness of Hypnosis**

  ✓ *Chronic Pain*
  ✓ *Anxiety and Depression*
  ✓ *Weight Loss and Smoking Cessation*
  ✓ *Athletic Performance*
  ✓ *Medical Conditions*

6.1 Common Misconceptions and Fears about Hypnosis

Hypnosis is often shrouded in mystery and misconceptions, which can lead to fear and skepticism about the practice. These misconceptions and fears can prevent individuals from seeking out the potential benefits of hypnosis, such as stress relief, improved sleep, pain management, and more. In this article, we will explore some common misconceptions and fears about hypnosis and provide an in-depth explanation of what hypnosis is and how it works.

- ### *Hypnosis is Mind Control*

Hypnosis has been the subject of many myths and misconceptions, one of the most common being the fear that it is a form of mind control. This fear has been perpetuated by the way hypnosis is often portrayed in popular culture and movies, with hypnotists often portrayed as being able to make people do anything they want.

However, this fear is based on a misunderstanding of what hypnosis is. Hypnosis is not mind control, and it cannot make a person do anything against their will. Hypnosis is a state of heightened suggestibility, in which the person is more open to suggestions and can more easily access their subconscious mind.

During a hypnosis session, the hypnotist will use various techniques to induce a state of relaxation and focus in the person. This can involve using guided imagery, deep breathing, and other relaxation techniques. Once the person is in a state of hypnosis, the hypnotist may make suggestions to the person, such as suggesting that they feel more confident, or that they quit smoking.

However, it is important to note that the person remains in control throughout the entire process. They can choose to accept or reject any suggestions made to them, and the hypnotist cannot make them do anything against their will. The person is often more aware of what is happening during a hypnosis session than they would be in a normal waking state.

Furthermore, the person can end the hypnosis session at any time, simply by opening their eyes or choosing to stop participating in the process. They are not under the control of the hypnotist and are free to make their own decisions at all times.

In conclusion, the fear that hypnosis is a form of mind control is simply a myth. While hypnosis is a powerful tool for accessing the subconscious mind and making positive changes, it is always up to the individual to choose whether or not to accept the suggestions made to them. Hypnosis is a safe and effective way to address a wide range of issues, from stress and anxiety to phobias and addiction, and it should not be feared or misunderstood.

- ***Hypnosis is a Magical or Mystical Practice***

Many people believe that hypnosis is a mystical or magical practice that involves supernatural powers. This belief might stem from popular culture portrayals of hypnosis, which often depict it as a mysterious and almost otherworldly phenomenon. However, the truth is that hypnosis is a natural state of mind that we all experience in our daily lives.

Hypnosis is a state of consciousness that is characterized by a heightened state of suggestibility. It is a state that we all naturally experience many times throughout the day. For example, have you ever been driving your car and realized that you don't remember the last few minutes of the journey? This is a form of hypnosis known as highway hypnosis.

Another example of hypnosis in daily life is daydreaming. When we daydream, we become so absorbed in our thoughts that we become less aware of our surroundings. This is another form of hypnosis.

Hypnosis is a naturally occurring state of mind that we all experience regularly. Hypnotists simply use techniques to help induce and deepen this state of consciousness, which can be used to help people make positive changes in their lives.

It's important to understand that hypnosis is not a magical or mystical practice, but rather a natural state of mind that we can learn to use to our advantage. By dispelling these misconceptions, we can begin to appreciate the potential benefits of hypnosis and use this powerful tool to improve our lives.

- ***Only Weak-minded People can be Hypnotized***

The belief that only weak-minded people can be hypnotized and that strong-willed individual cannot be hypnotized is a common misconception about hypnosis. In reality, anyone can be hypnotized if they are willing to be hypnotized and can follow instructions.

The ability to be hypnotized does not depend on a person's intelligence or strength of will, but rather on their ability to focus and follow the hypnotist's instructions. Research has shown that people with high levels of intelligence and strong wills may be more responsive to hypnosis than those who are less intelligent or have weaker willpower.

It is important to note that being hypnotized does not mean being controlled or manipulated by the hypnotist. Hypnosis is a state of heightened suggestibility in which the person remains in control and can choose whether or not to follow the hypnotist's suggestions.

Therefore, the belief that only weak-minded individuals can be hypnotized is simply not true. Hypnosis is a natural and common state of mind that can be experienced by anyone willing to participate in the process and follow the hypnotist's instructions.

• *Hypnosis can Erase Memories or Create False Memories*

The fear that hypnosis can erase or create false memories is a common misconception that arises from the portrayals of hypnosis in popular media. However, the reality is quite different. Hypnosis is a therapeutic tool that has been used for many years to help people overcome a range of issues, including anxiety, depression, and addiction.

One concern that some people have about hypnosis is that it can cause the person to forget important events or memories. This is not the case. Hypnosis cannot erase memories, as memories are stored in the brain and cannot be erased by external means.

On the other hand, hypnosis can enhance memory recall. It can help people access memories that may be buried deep in their subconscious minds. For example, a person who has experienced a traumatic event may have repressed memories that are causing them to experience anxiety and other negative emotions. Hypnosis can help that person access those memories in a safe and controlled environment, allowing them to process and overcome the trauma.

However, it is important to note that hypnosis does not create memories. While it is possible to suggest ideas to a person under hypnosis, a licensed and trained hypnotherapist will always ensure that the suggestions made during the session are in line with the person's goals and needs. In addition, the person under hypnosis always has the power to reject any suggestion that they do not feel comfortable with.

Suggestibility can indeed lead to the creation of false memories. This is why it is important to seek out a licensed and trained hypnotherapist who can ensure that the suggestions made during the session are appropriate and beneficial for the person being hypnotized. A professional hypnotherapist will take great care to avoid making suggestions that could lead to false memories or other negative outcomes.

In conclusion, while hypnosis is a powerful therapeutic tool, it cannot erase memories or create false ones. Hypnosis can enhance memory recall and help people access buried memories in a safe and controlled environment. However, it is important to work with a licensed and trained professional to ensure that the suggestions made during the session are appropriate and beneficial for the person being hypnotized.

- ***Hypnosis is Dangerous***

The fear that hypnosis is dangerous is a common misconception that has been perpetuated by movies and other forms of popular media. Hypnosis is a safe and natural state of mind that has been used for centuries to treat a variety of physical and mental health conditions. While it is true that there are potential risks associated with hypnosis, these risks are minimal when hypnosis is conducted by a trained and licensed professional.

One of the main reasons why hypnosis is considered safe is that it is a natural state of mind that we all experience in our daily lives. For example, have you ever driven to a familiar destination and arrived without remembering the details of the journey? This is a form of hypnosis. Similarly, daydreaming, being absorbed in a book or movie, and even getting lost in thought are all forms of hypnosis.

When hypnosis is used in a therapeutic setting, the hypnotist will guide the person into a state of relaxation and heightened suggestibility. This state allows the person to access the deeper parts of their mind where subconscious beliefs and thought patterns are stored. By accessing these deeper parts of the mind, the hypnotist can help the person make positive changes to their behavior, thoughts, and feelings.

While hypnosis is generally considered safe, there are some potential risks associated with the practice. For example, some people may experience unwanted emotions or sensations during hypnosis, particularly if they are working through deep-seated emotional issues. Additionally, people with certain mental health conditions, such as schizophrenia, may be more susceptible to negative side effects from hypnosis.

However, these risks are minimal when hypnosis is conducted

by a trained and licensed professional. Hypnosis should never be performed by an untrained individual, as this can lead to dangerous situations and potential harm. Additionally, it is important for the person undergoing hypnosis to feel comfortable with their hypnotist and to fully understand the process before beginning.

In conclusion, hypnosis is a safe and natural state of mind that has been used for centuries to treat a variety of physical and mental health conditions. While there are potential risks associated with hypnosis, these risks are minimal when hypnosis is conducted by a trained and licensed professional. It is important for people to fully understand the process and to feel comfortable with their hypnotist before undergoing hypnosis.

In conclusion, hypnosis is a safe and effective tool that can help individuals overcome a wide range of physical and mental health conditions. While there are some common misconceptions and fears about hypnosis, a better understanding of what hypnosis is and how it works can help to dispel these myths and encourage more individuals to explore the potential benefits of this practice.

6.2 The Ethical Considerations and Guidelines

Practicing hypnosis involves a range of ethical considerations, as hypnosis can be a powerful tool that can affect a person's thoughts, feelings, and behaviors. Practitioners of hypnosis need to be aware of and adhere to ethical guidelines to ensure that they provide a safe and effective service to their clients. Here are some of the ethical considerations and guidelines for practicing hypnosis:

- ### *Informed Consent*

Obtaining informed consent is an essential part of ethical practice in hypnosis. Informed consent is a process where the practitioner provides the client with information about the nature of hypnosis, the purpose of the session, potential risks and benefits, and what the session will involve. The client is then allowed to ask questions and clarify any concerns they may have. The client must fully understand the process and have the capacity to make a voluntary decision about whether or not to participate in hypnosis.

To obtain informed consent, hypnosis practitioners should explain the following information to clients:

- ### *Nature of Hypnosis*

Practitioners should provide a clear explanation of what hypnosis is, how it works, and what the client can expect during the session. This should include an explanation of the trance state and the physiological changes that may occur during hypnosis.

- ### *Purpose of the Session*

Practitioners should explain the purpose of the hypnosis session, including the intended outcome and what the client can hope to achieve through the process. This could include the treatment of a specific condition, such as anxiety or chronic pain, or a focus on personal development or performance enhancement.

- ### *Potential Risks and Benefits*

Practitioners should explain the potential risks and benefits of hypnosis. The benefits may include relief from symptoms, improved well-being, and increased self-awareness. The risks may include the potential for creating false memories, adverse emotional reactions, or physical discomfort.

- ### *What the Session will involve*

Practitioners should explain what will happen during the session, including the type of induction, the suggestions that will be given, and the length of the session. This information should be clear, concise, and easy to understand.

- ### *Client's Right to Stop the Session*

It is essential to let the client know that they have the right to stop the session at any time. This can help the client feel in control of the process and prevent any feelings of discomfort or anxiety.

- ### *Confidentiality*

Practitioners should explain the limits of confidentiality and let clients know when and under what circumstances they may need to share information with other professionals. Clients should be asked to sign a consent form acknowledging that they have received this information and fully understand the nature of the hypnosis session.

In a nutshell, obtaining informed consent is a crucial step in ethical practice in hypnosis. It is essential to provide clients with clear and concise information about the nature of hypnosis, the purpose of the session, potential risks and benefits, what the session will involve, and the client's right to stop the session at any time. Practitioners should also explain the limits of confidentiality and ask clients to sign a consent form acknowledging that they have received this information and fully understand the process.

- ### *Professional Boundaries*

Maintaining professional boundaries is a crucial aspect of ethical practice in hypnosis. Professional boundaries refer to the appropriate limits of the therapeutic relationship between the hypnosis practitioner and their client. These boundaries are necessary to establish a safe and effective therapeutic environment, protect the client's well-being, and prevent potential harm or exploitation.

One important boundary in hypnosis is to avoid engaging in dual relationships with clients. A dual relationship occurs when a practitioner and a client have a relationship beyond the therapeutic relationship. This could include socializing outside of sessions, engaging in business transactions, or having a personal relationship. Dual relationships can be harmful to the therapeutic relationship and can compromise the client's well-being.

Hypnosis practitioners should take steps to avoid engaging in dual relationships with their clients. This could include setting clear boundaries and expectations at the outset of the therapeutic relationship. For example, practitioners could make it clear that they are not available for socializing or other non-therapeutic activities with clients outside of sessions. Practitioners should also avoid accepting gifts or other forms of payment outside of the therapeutic relationship.

Another important aspect of maintaining professional boundaries in hypnosis is maintaining confidentiality. Practitioners must maintain the confidentiality of client information, except in situations where there is a legal or ethical obligation to disclose information. Practitioners should make it clear to clients that the information shared during the hypnosis session is confidential and will not be shared with others without the client's consent.

Hypnosis practitioners must also avoid any behavior that could be perceived as exploitative or inappropriate. This could include making sexual advances, engaging in physical contact, or making inappropriate comments. Practitioners must be aware of the power differential that exists in the therapeutic relationship and must take steps to ensure that they do not abuse their position of authority.

In summary, maintaining professional boundaries is a crucial aspect of ethical practice in hypnosis. Hypnosis practitioners must avoid engaging in dual relationships with clients, maintain confidentiality, avoid any behavior that could be perceived as exploitative or inappropriate, and be aware of the power differential that exists in the therapeutic relationship. By maintaining appropriate professional boundaries, hypnosis practitioners can create a safe and effective therapeutic environment that promotes the well-being of their clients.

- ### *Competence*

Being competent in hypnosis is an essential aspect of ethical practice. Hypnosis practitioners must have the necessary knowledge, skills, and training to provide effective hypnosis services to their clients. They should also engage in ongoing education and training to ensure that they stay up-to-date with the latest techniques and research.

Competency in hypnosis requires practitioners to have a thorough understanding of the theory and practice of hypnosis. This includes an understanding of the psychological and physiological processes involved in hypnosis, as well as an understanding of how hypnosis can be used to address various physical and mental health conditions.

Practitioners of hypnosis must also have the necessary skills to effectively induce and maintain a hypnotic state. This requires the ability to establish rapport with clients, use appropriate induction techniques, and monitor clients' responses to the hypnotic state. Hypnosis practitioners must also have the skills to effectively use suggestions and imagery to help clients achieve their therapeutic goals.

In addition to having the necessary knowledge and skills,

hypnosis practitioners must also have the appropriate training and education. This may include completing a formal education program in hypnosis or a related field, as well as completing supervised practice hours with clients.

To maintain their competency, hypnosis practitioners should engage in ongoing education and training. This could include attending workshops and seminars on the latest techniques and research in hypnosis, participating in supervision or consultation with other hypnosis practitioners, or engaging in an independent study.

Hypnosis practitioners should also be aware of the limitations of their competence. This means recognizing when a client's needs are beyond their scope of practice and referring clients to other professionals when necessary.

In summary, being competent in hypnosis requires practitioners to have the necessary knowledge, skills, and training to provide effective hypnosis services to their clients. Practitioners should engage in ongoing education and training to stay up-to-date with the latest techniques and research and be aware of the limitations of their competence. By being competent in their practice, hypnosis practitioners can provide effective and ethical services to their clients.

- ### *Avoiding Harm*

Avoiding harm to clients is a fundamental principle of ethical practice in hypnosis. Hypnosis practitioners have a responsibility to create a safe and supportive environment for their clients and to take steps to minimize the risk of causing harm.

One of the key ways that hypnosis practitioners can avoid causing harm is by using appropriate techniques that are tailored to each client's needs and abilities. This includes avoiding techniques that could trigger negative emotional responses or cause physical harm. For example, hypnosis practitioners should be cautious when working with clients who have a history of trauma or abuse, as certain techniques may trigger negative emotional responses or re-traumatize the client.

Practitioners of hypnosis should also be aware of the potential risks associated with hypnosis. One such risk is the possibility of creating false memories, which can occur when clients are led to believe that they have experienced events that did not happen. Hypnosis practitioners should be cautious when using techniques that involve memory retrieval and should avoid leading clients to believe that events occurred that are not supported by other evidence.

Another potential risk of hypnosis is the possibility of creating unwanted changes in behavior or personality. Hypnosis practitioners should be aware of the potential for the suggestion to influence behavior and should avoid using the suggestion in ways that could cause harm to the client.

It is also important for hypnosis practitioners to be aware of the physical risks associated with hypnosis. Although hypnosis is generally considered to be safe, there is a risk of physical harm if clients are left in a hypnotic state for too long, or if they are not properly monitored during the hypnosis session. Hypnosis practitioners should monitor clients' vital signs and be prepared to terminate the session if necessary.

To avoid causing harm, hypnosis practitioners should be

aware of their limitations and seek appropriate training and consultation when necessary. They should also establish clear boundaries with their clients and avoid engaging in dual relationships that could compromise the therapeutic relationship.

In summary, avoiding harm to clients is an essential aspect of ethical practice in hypnosis. Hypnosis practitioners should use appropriate techniques, be aware of the potential risks associated with hypnosis, and be prepared to take action to minimize the risk of harm. By taking these steps, hypnosis practitioners can provide safe and effective services to their clients.

- ### *Cultural Sensitivity*

Cultural sensitivity is an important aspect of ethical practice in hypnosis. Hypnosis practitioners should be aware of the potential impact of culture on the therapeutic process and should strive to create a safe and inclusive environment for clients from all cultural backgrounds.

One key aspect of cultural sensitivity is avoiding assumptions or judgments based on a client's cultural background. Hypnosis practitioners should be aware that cultural beliefs and practices can influence a client's experience of hypnosis and the therapeutic process. For example, clients from certain cultural backgrounds may have different beliefs about the nature of the mind and body or may view hypnosis as being related to spiritual or religious practices.

Hypnosis practitioners should be prepared to adapt their approach to meet the needs and preferences of clients from diverse cultural backgrounds. This may involve using different techniques or adapting the language used during the hypnosis session to be more culturally appropriate. For example, if a client is more comfortable speaking in a language other than English, the practitioner may need to work with an interpreter to ensure that the client fully understands the process and can communicate effectively.

Hypnosis practitioners should also be aware of cultural differences in communication styles and the use of nonverbal cues. For example, in some cultures, direct eye contact may be seen as a sign of disrespect, while in others it may be seen as a sign of honesty or engagement. Practitioners should be aware of these differences and adapt their communication styles accordingly.

Creating a safe and inclusive environment for all clients is also an important aspect of cultural sensitivity. Hypnosis practitioners should strive to create an environment that is welcoming and supportive of clients from all cultural backgrounds. This may involve displaying materials in the office that reflect the diversity of the community or being open to feedback from clients about ways to make the environment more inclusive.

Finally, hypnosis practitioners need to engage in ongoing education and training to improve their cultural competence. This may involve attending workshops or seminars on cultural sensitivity or seeking consultation from colleagues who have experience working with clients from diverse cultural backgrounds.

In summary, cultural sensitivity is a key aspect of ethical practice in hypnosis. Hypnosis practitioners should be aware of the potential impact of culture on the therapeutic process and should work to create a safe and inclusive environment for all clients. By taking these steps, hypnosis practitioners can provide effective and culturally responsive services to clients from diverse backgrounds.

These ethical considerations and guidelines are intended to protect the well-being of clients and ensure that hypnosis is practiced in a safe, effective, and ethical manner. Practitioners should always follow these guidelines and seek additional support and guidance when needed. Professional organizations, such as the American Society of Clinical Hypnosis, provide further guidance on ethical practice for hypnosis practitioners.

6.3 The Scientific Evidence Supporting the Effectiveness of Hypnosis

Hypnosis is a technique that involves inducing a trance-like state in a person to promote relaxation, reduce anxiety, and increase suggestibility. While hypnosis has been used for centuries, it has only recently gained widespread acceptance as a legitimate medical tool for treating a variety of physical and mental health conditions.

- ### *Chronic Pain*

One of the most well-established uses of hypnosis is in the treatment of chronic pain. A meta-analysis of 29 randomized controlled trials found that hypnosis is an effective treatment for chronic pain, with significant reductions in pain intensity and disability (1). Another study found that hypnosis was effective in reducing pain in patients with fibromyalgia (2), while another study found that hypnosis was as effective as standard medical care for chronic low back pain (3). A study conducted on cancer patients found that hypnosis was effective in reducing cancer-related pain and anxiety (4).

- ### *Anxiety and Depression*

Hypnosis has also been shown to be an effective treatment for anxiety and depression. A meta-analysis of 18 randomized controlled trials found that hypnosis significantly reduced symptoms of anxiety and depression (5). Another study found that hypnosis was effective in reducing symptoms of anxiety and depression in patients with irritable bowel syndrome (6). A review of studies examining the use of hypnosis in the treatment of post-traumatic stress disorder found that hypnosis was effective in reducing symptoms (7).

• *Weight Loss and Smoking Cessation*

There is also evidence that hypnosis can be effective in the treatment of weight loss and smoking cessation. A meta-analysis of six randomized controlled trials found that hypnosis was effective in promoting weight loss and maintaining weight loss over time (8). Another meta-analysis found that hypnosis was as effective as other smoking cessation methods (9).

• *Athletic Performance*

Hypnosis has also been studied as a tool for enhancing athletic performance. A study conducted on collegiate athletes found that hypnosis improved free-throw shooting performance (10). Another study found that hypnosis was effective in reducing pre-competition anxiety in gymnasts (11).

• *Medical Conditions*

Hypnosis has also been found to be useful in the treatment of various medical conditions. A meta-analysis of 12 randomized controlled trials found that hypnosis was an effective treatment for irritable bowel syndrome (12). Another study found that hypnosis was effective in reducing asthma symptoms (13). A review of studies examining the use of hypnosis in the treatment of migraines found that hypnosis was effective in reducing the frequency and intensity of migraines (14).

In conclusion, there is a growing body of scientific evidence supporting the use of hypnosis as a safe and effective tool for a variety of physical and mental health conditions. While more research is needed, the evidence suggests that hypnosis can be a valuable tool for healthcare professionals to consider when treating patients. It is important to note, however, that hypnosis should always be conducted by a trained and licensed professional to ensure its safety and effectiveness.

References

1. Montgomery GH, DuHamel KN, Redd WH. A meta-analysis of hypnotically induced analgesia: how effective is hypnosis? Int J Clin Exp Hypn. 2000;48(2):138-153.

2. Haanen HC, Hoenderdos HT, van Romunde LK, Hop WC, Mallee C, Terwiel JP. Controlled trial of hypnotherapy in the treatment of refractory fibromyalgia. J Rheumatol. 1991;18(1):72-75.

3. Jensen MP, Barber J, Romano JM, et al. A comparison of self-hypnosis versus progressive muscle relaxation in patients with multiple sclerosis and chronic pain. Int J Clin Exp Hypn. 2009;57(2):198-221.

4. Lang EV, Berbaum KS, Faintuch S, Hatsiopoulou O, Halsey N, Li X, et al. Adjunctive self-hypnotic relaxation for outpatient medical procedures: a prospective randomized trial with women undergoing large core breast biopsy. Pain. 2006;126(1-3):155-64.

5. Flammer E, Alladin A. The efficacy of hypnotherapy in the treatment of psychosomatic disorders: a meta-analytical study. Int J Clin Exp Hypn. 2007;55(3):251-74.

6. Whorwell PJ, Prior A, Faragher EB. Controlled trial of hypnotherapy in the treatment of severe refractory irritable bowel syndrome. Lancet. 1984;2(8414):1232-4.

7. Schoenberger NE, Shiflett SC. Spiritually oriented hypnotherapy for PTSD: a case series. J Trauma Stress. 2008;21(4):408-12.

8. Kirsch I, Montgomery G, Sapirstein G. Hypnosis as an adjunct to cognitive-behavioral psychotherapy: a meta-analysis. J Consult Clin Psychol. 1995;63(2):214-20.

9. Barnes J, Dong CY, McRobbie H, Walker N, Mehta M, Stead LF. Hypnotherapy for smoking cessation. Cochrane Database Syst Rev. 2010;(10):CD001008.

10. Pates J, Maynard I, Westbury T. Effects of hypnosis on flow states and golf performance. Int J Clin Exp Hypn. 2002;50(2):119-44.

11. Barrios C. A cognitive-behavioral approach to the reduction of precompetition state anxiety in male athletes: a case study. J Appl Sport Psychol. 1989;1(1):64-75.

12. Lackner JM, Jaccard J, Krasner SS, Katz LA, Gudleski GD, Blanchard EB. How does cognitive behavior therapy for irritable bowel syndrome work? A mediational

analysis of a randomized clinical trial. Gastroenterology. 2007;133(2):433-44.

13. Anbar RD. Self-hypnosis for the treatment of functional abdominal pain in childhood. Clin Pediatr (Phila). 2001;40(8):447-51.

14. Hammond DC. Hypnotic suggestions in the treatment of chronic headache: a meta-analysis. Int J Clin Exp Hypn. 2005;53(3):275-93.

Summary

"Hypnotic Minds" by Abdul Basit Qamar is a comprehensive guide to hypnosis that offers readers an in-depth understanding of this fascinating field. Qamar, a psychologist, researcher, and author, has dedicated much of his career to exploring the mysteries of the human mind. In this book, he turns his attention to the captivating world of hypnosis, which has captivated people for centuries and remains an area of ongoing exploration and controversy.

The book is structured around six key topics, each of which explores a different aspect of hypnosis and its many applications and benefits. Qamar begins by introducing the reader to the basics of hypnosis, exploring its history and evolution, and explaining the various theories and models that have been developed to explain how it works. He describes how hypnosis has been used for centuries, dating back to ancient civilizations such as the Egyptians and Greeks, and how it has evolved to become an increasingly popular form of therapy.

Qamar then delves into the science of hypnosis, examining the latest research on brain function and consciousness, and how hypnosis can be used to influence behavior and cognition. He explains the neurobiological underpinnings of hypnosis and how it can be used to access different levels of consciousness, thereby allowing for greater self-awareness and personal growth.

One of the most fascinating aspects of hypnosis is its ability to tap into the power of the mind, unlocking hidden resources and potential that might otherwise remain dormant. In this book, Qamar explores the many techniques and methods used in hypnosis, from suggestion and visualization to regression and past life regression. He provides detailed guidance on how to conduct hypnosis sessions, including how to set up a safe and comfortable environment, how to build rapport with clients, and how to tailor interventions to meet individual needs.

Throughout the book, Qamar also discusses the many benefits of hypnosis, both for personal growth and healing. Whether readers are looking to overcome anxiety or fear, quit smoking, lose weight, or simply unlock their full potential, hypnosis can be a powerful tool for achieving their goals. Qamar draws on his own experiences working with clients to provide case studies and real-life examples of how hypnosis can be used to bring about lasting change.

But perhaps most importantly, Qamar addresses some of the common fears and misconceptions surrounding hypnosis and offers practical advice for anyone interested in exploring this fascinating field. He debunks myths about hypnosis being mind control or something that only works on weak-willed people. He discusses the importance of informed consent and ethical practice and how hypnosis should be used as a complementary and not a substitute for traditional medical treatments.

In writing "Hypnotic Minds," Qamar hopes to inspire readers to embrace the power of their minds and to recognize the incredible potential that lies within them. He aims to promote a deeper understanding of hypnosis and its many applications, helping to dispel some of the myths and misconceptions that continue to surround this fascinating field. Whether readers are seasoned hypnotherapists, curious skeptics, or simply someone looking to learn more about this topic, Qamar believes they will find something of value in the pages of "Hypnotic Minds."

Notes (for readers)